Great Opens

GREAT OPENS

Historic British and American
Championships 1913–1975

Michael Hobbs
with a foreword by Henry Cotton

DAVID & CHARLES
NEWTON ABBOT   LONDON
NORTH POMFRET (VT)   VANCOUVER

ISBN 0 7153 7139 8
Library of Congress Catalog Card Number 76–7091

Set in 12 on 13pt Bembo
and printed in Great Britain
by Latimer Trend & Company Ltd Plymouth
for David & Charles (Publishers) Limited
Brunel House   Newton Abbot   Devon

Published in the United States of America
by David & Charles Inc
North Pomfret   Vermont 05053   USA

Published in Canada
by Douglas David & Charles Limited
1875 Welch Street   North Vancouver   BC

Contents

CONTENTS

Foreword

GOLF has for long been fortunate in its reporters. Many of them exemplify journalism at its best, sometimes even crossing the divide between top-class newspaper writing and literature. I think it an excellent idea to recapture, as Michael Hobbs has done, the skill and excitement of some of the great Open Championships, because it puts the development of the game into perspective. As its popularity increases all over the world, all the more do great players emerge, and it would seem that never before have we had so many 'giants' at one time. It is salutary, therefore, to be reminded that, even with less effective clubs and balls, players like Francis Ouimet – as long ago as 1913 when he was only twenty – achieved remarkable rounds and defeated two of the champions of the day, Ted Ray and Harry Vardon, who were touring America at the time. The American Open Championship, as Michael Hobbs points out, was actually postponed for a month that year to enable these two British players to compete. Times have changed!

Inevitably, owing to the richness of golf history, Mr Hobbs has had to be selective, and he rightly concentrates on the past two decades. No such history could be complete, however, without Bobby Jones, the first and only golfer to pull off the 'Grand Slam' by winning the Amateur and Open Championships of America and Great Britain in one year. Of course he is in, as is Gene Sarazen for his fine win in 1932 when he received a ticker-tape welcome in New York after taking the British Open. I myself am naturally gratified to be included too.

Only those who have won these great titles appreciate the agony of 'hanging on', as the pressure mounts in the closing holes of these 'fame and fortune' events. Being runner up is no good: nobody cares who is second.

Luck comes into golf and a one-time winner is duly acclaimed.

But those who can do it again join the élite and there have been four- and five-time winners, though these are very rare. Some Opens are 'won' (by a player in the lead throughout), but more are lost by those in a winning position who let the lead slip away, often by an odd stroke. In this lies all the drama of the Opens, so well told here.

Winning changes the life of the lucky ones; they have 'qualified' and become Master Golfers, and no matter how much or how little money they can pick up to add to the now substantial prize money, they have made it. My own life changed, for, besides achieving an ambition, my triumph put an extra shine on my game and my status.

All in all, *Great Opens* portrays the drama and strain of the international golf circuit today as well as the beauty of the play; moreover, as all true golfers know, the game has its moments of 'poetry', and this element too is nicely present.

HENRY COTTON
New Golf Club
Sotogrande
Prov Cadiz
Spain

February 1976

Introduction

WHEN I set out to write this book, there were several questions I had to ask myself. The most pressing was, obviously enough, what *is* a great Open Championship? I'm not sure that I found a complete answer, and the nearest I came to it was to discover that each of my instinctive choices usually contained one – or more – of several elements.

Difficult though they are to pin down, this is what they came to:

1   The winner slices through the field in his final round, having been in a near-hopeless position before.

2   The reverse situation, in which a golfer establishes dominance during the first three rounds and then, the prize in his palms, begins to stumble. Sometimes he picks himself up again (Cotton, 1934), sometimes not (Yancey, 1968).

3   The one-sided championship. On the face of it there is a lack of drama when a man leads from start to finish and at no time falters seriously, but when you get down to the details it becomes apparent that each nearly let it slip away at some stage (Jacklin, 1970, Palmer, 1962), even though the final scores show a wide gap between first and second. Anyway, there is also the experience of seeing a man at the summit of the practice of his craft.

4   The championship in which the leadership changes hands from round to round and from hole to hole.

5   An unknown takes the title and humbles the mighty (Fleck, 1955). This is not nearly so dramatic, of course, if unknown beats unknown (Lou Graham and John Mahaffey, 1975).

But all this is only the 'plot' of an Open Championship story. The characters are more important still, because how we feel about them controls our response to their victories and defeats. For this reason I have written also about championships that do

9

not fall into any of the categories above. That Roberto de Vicenzo won the 1967 British Open after so many years of being close is, in itself, most of the story of that year's championship. Perhaps, indeed, the character and career of the winner – and some of the losers – is always every bit as significant as the particular dramatic framework of an Open.

An Open can also be seen as great because it marked the arrival of a great golfer (Vardon, 1896) or was the culmination of one golfer's life, Thomson in 1965, for example. If, however, a golfer won but a single Open and then merged into obscurity once more, we are unlikely to remember 'his' year vividly, unless there is the poignancy of someone such as Jack Fleck improbably beating the great Hogan.

Alert and knowledgeable readers may spot the odd error of fact or interpretation; there is one of etiquette that I admit to now. There is no such event as the *British* Open. It is, of course, quite simply, 'The Open'. I felt, however, that retaining this usage would create confusion in a book dealing with Open Championships held in both Britain and the USA. My calling one the 'British Open' does not have the intention of renaming so venerable an institution; the idea was just to keep the geography clear.

Finally, the reader may feel that too much space has been allowed the British Open as compared to the US Open and that there are gaps in time. I have written very little, for example, about the Opens of the first quarter of this century and earlier, nor of the 1935–52 period. I felt that a great Open has to have a great field. Of the two championships, the British does, and did, attract more talent from outside than the American competition, but there have been periods of time when both events were parochial. There was a good American attendance in Britain during the 1920s and early 1930s, which then lapsed until Arnold Palmer revived American interest after 1960. Few British players contest the US Open – alas since World War I only one or two players of any era would have had a chance – and the British Open secures a very good entry from the rest of the world. Despite these arguments, however, a number of US

Opens would force their inclusion in any collection of the kind I have attempted. And what of the 1965 US Open! Gary Player, South Africa, first; Kel Nagle, Australia, second. A blow for American nationalism of a kind that British feelings have long since learnt to tolerate.

Mastery

The man who nearly threw it all away - the 1934 British Open

HENRY COTTON arrived for the championship with four sets of clubs and a greater number of problems with his swing. He tried each set of clubs; he tried the variations of swing – the left thumb here, the right little finger a little more snugly fitted to the left hand, more of a pause at the top, lower through the ball. It was all really quite hopeless. In the end he threw his clubs into the back of the car on the Saturday before the Monday's qualifying round and drove away. However, now that he was there, it seemed he might as well play.

On Monday he played just about the best round of golf of his life for a 66. This was two strokes under a course record that had stood for no less than twenty years. There must be a moral somewhere. Perhaps it is that the swinging hit of a golf stroke must be timed so perfectly that the margins between a superb shot, a moderate one, and a quick slice or low, rapidly curling hook are very fine indeed. On that Monday it all suddenly came right. For the second qualifying round he was able to amble round Deal in a relaxed mood.

For the first round proper, back on the championship course at Royal St Georges, Sandwich, he was paired with Marcel Dallemagne, France's finest golfer. For a while it was a match-play event, as first Dallemagne birdied the 1st and Cotton the 2nd, after he had nearly driven the green. So they went on. At the 5th Dallemagne holed a long putt, but Cotton chipped in. After holing virtually nothing but putting everything stone dead, Cotton was out in 31, with Dallemagne still only two shots behind him. At the 11th Cotton made the mistake of driving too far and too straight, finding a bunker placed to catch the second

shot, and so conceded his only bogey of the round. He finished
in 67; Dallemagne had a 71. Second place, however, was held
by Taggart, a little-known golfer who recorded a 70. Apparently
he had not played any too well, but it is difficult to have a really
bad score if you take only 20 putts! He did not the next day ...

Also in with 71s were the holder, Densmore Shute, and
Cotton's closest rival for the unofficial title of best British golfer,
Alfred Padgham. Sarazen, winner in 1932, had done no better
than 75.

The next day Cotton went to work again, and gave a name to
a golf ball – the Dunlop '65'. He pitched dead for a birdie on the
2nd, made his one error on the 8th, where he pushed a shot into
a bunker for a bogey and reached the turn in 33. He came back
in one less, finishing with three consecutive 3s. There was no 5
on his card.

He had now established a massive lead. From 132, there was a
gap of nine shots between Cotton and Padgham. Then came
C. A. Whitcombe, Shute and the trick-shot expert, Joe Kirkwood, all on 143.

Conditions were sterner on the final day, for there was a stiff
north-westerly breeze. Cotton's scoring was not as good and he
actually committed human errors, fluffing a chip once and
socketing. With his 72, however, he lost little ground over anyone in the field and increased his lead over the second-place
holder. The position was Cotton, 204; Kirkwood, 214; Dallemagne, 215; Padgham, 216. Even one of Sarazen's celebrated
charges would give him no chance of pulling up from 222.

A good crowd gathered to follow home the potential first
British winner of the Open since Arthur Havers. That was part
of the trouble. Cotton was delayed in teeing off for some fifteen
minutes while the stewards controlled the crowd. Those near to
him remarked that he looked rather green and Cotton later said
that he was suffering from stomach cramp.

Nevertheless he eventually got a good drive away, but three
strokes later he was still about 4yd from the hole. Never mind,
the putt went in. On the next he missed his drive and this time
was 10yd from the hole in three. Again the putt went down.

When he parred the next two the crisis seemed past, whereupon he promptly hooked into a sand crater and took 6. A bogey followed on the 6th and at last his putter failed to save him when he three-putted the 7th. To complete the first half he hit three bad shots and was still short of the 9th green, but then managed to struggle down in two more. So, out in 40. It could have been a great deal worse, but it would be more difficult to better that total on the second nine for three of the short holes were past.

Cotton set out back with a salvo of 5s and reached the 13th tee knowing that he needed 83 to win. Sid Brews, after a poor first round, had followed with three good ones to set the target at 288. The questions had now changed. It was no longer 'would Cotton beat Sarazen's record of 283?' or 'how many would he win by?' and 'who would be second?' It looked now as if he would have to play very good golf over the last holes to even win.

On the 13th, a par 5, he hit a good drive, was quite near the green with his second, and then chipped to 10ft. The putt went in for a birdie. On the instant, Cotton returned to the brand of golf he had been playing all week. He was on each green in the regulation number of strokes and each time he putted up dead. On the 15th, 16th and 17th he came very close to birdies. He finished in 79 and a total of 283. The championship cup stayed in Britain for the first time in eleven years.

Cotton's win, and perhaps the fact that he had three times beaten the previous course record to do it, did a great deal for British golf. From then until World War II no American won the championship, as other British players of the day – such as Padgham, Whitcombe, Perry, Burton and Cotton again – took the Open. Cotton had shown that British golf was not dead and that in him the country had arguably the finest golfer in the world. This belief was strengthened three years later when the Ryder Cup was played in Britain. All the US team entered at Carnoustie, and names such as Snead, Byron Nelson, Horton Smith and Ralph Guldahl all finished a long way behind him.

Henry Cotton's victory, and continuing dominance into the 1950s, had another effect on the British professional golf scene that was no less significant than the quality of his play. Hagen, in the USA, had been the first golfer to secure really high earnings. As he said, although he did not want to be a millionaire, he did want to live like one. Cotton, despite not having a flamboyant personality to match Hagen's, carried through the same role in Britain. He had wanted to charge high fees for lessons and exhibitions and felt that a professional golfer was undervalued. But it had not been enough merely to be thought the best British golfer. You had to win the Open. Before he did that, his driving around in the magnificence of a Mercedes sports car had been seen as evidence that Cotton thought far too much of himself, while having far too little in the way of achievements to his credit. Several times in the British Open he had been in contention, only to fade away in the last round. After 1934 he was able to make the money he thought his excellence as a golfer merited, and others in his profession benefited – if not equally – from this. Only Cotton, however, was offered a variety theatre contract during which he demonstrated his mastery to all and sundry on the stage of the London Palladium. As in golf, he was top of the bill.

One man in it - the 1962 British Open

For a good many years the British Open had been the personal preserve of Bobby Locke and Peter Thomson. Since World War II only Fred Daly, Max Faulkner and Henry Cotton had taken it amongst the British players, and this despite the absence of formidable US challenges. When a top American had come, as often or not he had left with the trophy. Worse, such was the lack of prestige of the Open that the Americans had often not bothered to return to defend the championship the year following a victory. Snead and Hogan did not come back after their successes in 1946 and 1953. Apparently it was good for the reputation to win the British Open once but neither the ego nor reputation demanded a second victory.

Palmer had changed all that. After a dramatic fight to the finish with Kel Nagle at St Andrews in 1960, when he had come second, he had taken the championship at Royal Birkdale the following year and was back to defend it. Palmer's interest had stirred the interest of other world-class golfers and over the years this was to lead to the British Open becoming once again what it now is – the most coveted title of them all.

The field for the 1962 Open was the strongest since the whole US Ryder Cup team had played at Carnoustie in 1937. Just about everyone who had won it since the war was there. Even Snead had overcome his distaste for what he called 'camping out' in Britain. In addition there was the man with the peerless swing, the 1961 US Open Champion, Gene Littler, and there was also a young man who had been a professional for just six months but was fresh from beating Palmer in a play-off for the 1962 US Open and who had won money in each of the US tournaments he had entered. Jack Nicklaus, without doubt at twenty-two the best young golfer since Bobby Jones, was already chasing a kind of mini Grand Slam. Holder of both the US Open and Amateur, the British would round things off very tidily.

Troon that year was both a severe and slightly unfair test of a golfer. It was long – over 7,000yd – with ten holes of 400yd or more, and the greens were small. Unfortunately it was baked hard in the drought and too much depended on the luck or bad luck of the bounce. You could skip sideways off a fairway after a perfect drive, and of two similar long irons, one might bite and stop near the flag while another would hit a hard knob and finish yards through the green. The greens themselves were a little below championship standard and played unevenly. The winner would have to prove himself able to keep his composure when fate was against him. Some failed to do this, and even failed to qualify.

In 1962 it was still necessary to qualify. Any club professional could enter. This meant that a great number with no hope of qualifying, let alone finishing well up the field, entered because they wanted to see the championship. The qualifying rounds produced no great surprises. Snead led at Troon with a 69 while Palmer caused himself some anxious moments by taking a 76, but he found fewer problems when he moved over to an easier nearby course for the second qualifying round.

It is usual for an unknown to lead the Open after the first round proper and the 1962 was no exception. At the end of the first day K. A. Macdonald was a shot in the lead with a 69. Of those believed to have a real chance, some were already gone, for no one had won an Open with a 77 since Walter Hagen in the 1920s.

Many observers felt that the 11th might be the key to the championship. It was a double dog-leg, with a long, long stretch of savage rough between tee and fairway. This curved first to the left and then right towards the green. All along on the right was an out-of-bounds railway line which was still with the players when they arrived at the long and narrow green. The way to play the hole was to drive over the angle of the first dog-leg, undeterred by the waist-high gorse, after which you had to stop the ball within about 30yd on the hard and bald fairway. After that, there remained a perilous 200yd passage between the gorse. In a stiff cross wind some players were to find the hole almost unplayable, Troon's Becher's Brook. It marked the end of Nicklaus's first Grand Slam attempt. He came in with an 80 that included a 10 on this hole. He was not alone in being in double figures.

Bobby Locke and Gene Littler did little better with 78 and 79 and Snead – everyone was saying he was too old anyway (as they still are) – had not managed the good start he needed. A 76 was probably just a couple of shots too many. There had been no real British hopes that year, and perhaps only Peter Alliss and David Thomas, both long and straight drivers, were given any sort of a chance. Theirs too had gone when they posted 77s.

But the man who had made the British Open almost his own personal property had rejoiced, as usual, in the particular problems of playing a bone-hard links course where those who played target golf were at a disadvantage. Thomson was and is a master of the 'made-up' shot. Not, for example, hitting a 6-iron full out at the flag but rather taking a half 2-iron and letting it drift in on the wind, or consistently playing a skipping run-up with a 5-iron over the bumps and hollows, instead of wedging directly at the pin.

Thomson loves neither Americans nor the kind of golf they play, and no doubt he was pleased with his 70 which made him the leader amongst those with a chance of winning. Close behind with 71s came two recent winners, Arnold Palmer and Kel Nagle. Gary Player, protesting his dislike of the course, had a 74, and on 75 were Phil Rodgers, an American, Bob Charles and Brian Huggett.

In retrospect, the second round well-nigh decided the championship. Thomson had a 77 and Palmer moved two shots into the lead. He had struggled out to the turn in 37, still bothered by the greens, and had then come home in 32. Only Nagle was still well within reach with a second 71. For a while Peter Alliss had roused British hopes with one of those great rounds that got away. He was out in 32 and had had six birdies and pars on all the rest after thirteen holes. A 66 or less seemed well within his powers. But a couple of putts slipped away and he plugged in the vertical face of a bunker on the 16th. In the end it was no better than a 69 – still the best round of the championship at that time.

As in the Centenary Open at St Andrews two years before, it seemed to be a contest between the slashing abandon of Palmer and the imperturbable tidiness of Kel Nagle around the greens. Two ahead when they went out, Palmer had lost them both after four holes and was now in fact one stroke behind Nagle. But the 4th and the 11th were key holes for Palmer throughout this Open. The 11th was the hole he consistently played superbly, thrashing 1- and 2-irons boldly through the whins at the green. The 4th he played badly until the final round. It was, in fact, the hole that made him hitch up his pants in that characteristic way and go for everything in the remainder of the round. Today, everyone is ready for a dramatic last-round burst from Miller or Nicklaus. Palmer is more likely to begin a round well and perhaps fade on the run-in, but in 1962 he was at a peak of confidence. If he began a round badly then he would have to defy fate and hit every iron full at the flag and go boldly for every putt.

From the 4th hole onwards Palmer played the round of his life. He may have frequently scored lower, but perhaps never on a course quite as daunting as Troon that year. Although it was on the first four holes – three not overlong par 4s and a par 5 – that players felt they had the best chance to pick up a couple of birdies, it was the remainder of the course that Palmer plundered. From the 5th to the 18th he was seven under 4s and finished with a 67.

At lunchtime only Nagle was still in sight of the leader. He had added a 70 to his previous pair of 71s and stood five shots behind on 212. With nothing better than third place to hope for were Charles, 215, Rodgers, 217 and Thomas, 218. A few shots further out came Snead, Thomson, Alliss and Huggett.

Any leader beginning his final round, especially if his lead is a commanding one, must be prey to doubts. Had not Cotton, nine strokes in front, gone out in 40 in his final round in 1934 and followed that up with three 5s? If Palmer had any such fears on this occasion, however, they were not apparent. For a change, it was the first nine holes that he dealt with most severely, even reaching the 580yd 6th in two, to go out in 33. The rest was a triumphal progress, made chaotic by crowd control so ineffectual that it did at least ensure that British Opens would henceforth be competently organised. Palmer finished his second round of the day under 70 – a 69 this time – and Nagle again held on to record a repeat 70.

What people who saw Palmer in 1962 remember most is the power of his driving and the effectiveness of his long irons. It was certainly his strength and verve with the latter that did most to win him the championship. He was also at a peak of confidence in his putting stroke.

Today, however, even the bare statistics can enable us to picture his mastery. There were seven rounds better than 70 in the championship proper. Three of these were Palmer's. His winning total, 276, was a record and his six-stroke margin was the biggest since Hagen's in 1929. Nicklaus, new rival to his dominance on the American circuit, finished 29 strokes behind, and Nagle's considerable achievement of keeping in touch until near the end was emphasised by the third placing; Huggett, although he made his last round his best with a 69, still finished 13 shots worse than Palmer. British golf had to take what consolation it could from that. There was little else to boast about with overseas players taking six of the first seven places! Palmer was now the crowned king on both sides of the Atlantic – and indeed wherever else he cared to play. Strangely though he was never again to take an Open Championship field by the scruff of the neck and shake it to pieces.

Love story - the 1927 British Open

Whenever Bobby Jones entered a tournament, the contest automatically became one of Jones *v* the field. Consider for a moment his record in the US Open alone. From 1922 to 1930 he finished first, tied first, or runner-up every year except 1927. In that year he won the British Open instead. Such then was his brilliance and consistency that his contemporaries, both the players and those who watched him, thought of him as a mechanical golfer so that, when his reputation had reached a peak in 1926, one finds that writers of the day show a strong tendency to refer only to his bad shots – they found them that unusual.

Jones was not a mechanical golfer at all; on the contrary, he was perhaps the most natural player that the game has known. He practised it is true, but hardly much more than a high-handicap player, and for him there was never the tournament build-up over the weeks and months before a major championship. Jones, as a true amateur, had a legal practice to run, and competed in run-of-the-mill tournaments on rare occasions only. He mainly depended, to keep in practice, on playing friendly fourballs – during the golf season only – at his home course.

During a championship there was nothing mechanical about his temperament. He played always in a high state of nervous tension which, as a teenager, was vented by outbursts of temper – always directed only against himself – and by club-throwing. In his prime, the tension found out his digestion: he could never

23

keep a meal down between rounds and lost pounds of weight during a championship week.

His play, despite what his contemporaries thought, seldom approached perfection. After retiring in 1930 at the age of twenty-eight, Jones always had one regret, he felt that he had never succeeded in seizing a formidable lead and then inexorably increasing it. Usually, if he managed the first of these tasks, the mechanism would let him down and he would squander shots over the 100yd or so in to the green. Jones himself said that until towards the end of his championship career this was indeed his Achilles' Heel, and it seemed to affect him more the better his position in the tournament was.

As regards the rest of his game, 'mechanical', as a descriptive term, is less wide of the mark. He was a magnificently straight driver and about as long as anyone could be with hickory-shafted clubs. His long-iron play was almost equally outstanding. With Walter Hagen, he was the best putter of his day on the green – and perhaps the best approach putter there has ever been. He did not in the least depend on some tirelessly practised method, but on touch and feel. Indeed he was fully prepared to shift his stance – and even his grip – in accordance with what happened to feel comfortable on the day.

From his seven Open wins one could select any one of them as a classic in its way, but I have singled out his 1927 victory at St Andrews – because of what went before and followed after, and because the manner of the winning reflects what I have so far had to say about him.

Bobby Jones first came to St Andrews in 1921 at the age of nineteen. Although he had yet to win any major championship at that time, he carried the reputation of being the best of American golfers and was by no means young in championship experience. He had first competed in the US Amateur at the age of fourteen and had performed very competently both then and since.

After two rounds, he had the respectable total of 151. Then, in strong winds, the machine broke down in more ways than one. He went out in 46, followed that with a 6 and then put a shot into Hill Bunker. What happened then is still a matter of dispute: some say he teed up his ball and drove it into the river Eden; Jones claimed that it was his torn-up card only which he threw in that direction while the ball went into his pocket. But he learned a lesson and made a resolution. Such was the shame he felt that he vowed never again to allow his temper off a tight rein. No one thereafter was known to accuse him of anything more violent than a frown.

Jones returned to St Andrews six years later as holder of the British Open, which he had won the previous year at Royal Lytham and St Annes before recrossing the Atlantic to pick up the US title as well. The field was not a strong one and, as had now become usual, none doubted that Jones would be the winner – except for Jones himself. True there were big names in plenty but in the main they were the names of men with a past or a future. The Great Triumvirate were there, Harry Vardon, James Braid and John Henry Taylor, but all three had been competing in Opens for more than a quarter of a century and were in their fifties. In the same category was a fourth famous name, Ted Ray, although he was a few years younger. Of those with a future, the twenty-year-old Henry Cotton had already attracted critical esteem, but his prime lay ahead in the 1930s.

The main threat, if any, was expected from one of the more recent winners – George Duncan, Jim Barnes, Arthur Havers or perhaps one of the Whitcombe brothers. Two of the greatest of English amateurs, Cyril Tolley and Roger Wethered, were also given some chance, as was Wild Bill Mehlhorn.

In the first qualifying round Jones, suffering from lack of touch in his putting, had to be content with a 76, but in the second round he started holing the ones he had been sending trickling past and recorded a 71. His total of 147 put him in fourth place. Cyril Tolley had shown good form, going round in 73 in the first round, after taking an extravagant four putts on the last green, and 71 in the second. But no one remembers who led the qualifiers and Tolley faded when the championship proper began.

Jones, on the other hand, seemed to have won the thing with

his first round. His 68 equalled the course record, put him four strokes ahead of anyone else, and a good few more ahead of his most-favoured rivals. Joe Kirkwood followed with 72, Percy Alliss and Cotton were 73, Braid, at fifty-seven years of age, had 75, and Barnes and Taylor were on 76.

It has been said that the course was easy, that St Andrews was not as difficult as it once had been. (They are saying this today even more than ever – a comment on the difficulty of courses of the past as opposed to the present.) Apparently the greens fell short by not being glassy and, heresy, you didn't have to play a pitch and run to them. They were sufficiently holding for the then despised pitch shot to stick. Furthermore, from the first day until the end of the week there was never more than a light easterly breeze, and St Andrews, like most linksland courses, needs a wind to make it a fully valid championship test.

However, if you consider that a 76 was good enough for fourth place, most of the field obviously had not come near Jones's haul of birdies. He had perhaps been fired by a poor start – this usually brought the best out of him. On the 2nd he had failed to get out of a bunker at the first attempt and had saved himself from a double bogey only by a long putt. Thereafter his putter worked well and his long game was magnificent – he alone was reaching the par 5s in two. He holed from 35yd on the 5th, 6ft on the next and then swept one in from 5yd for a 2 on the 8th. He was out in 32 and had taken but seven putts on six consecutive greens. His return was less inspired, marred to some extent by his being short with a couple of pitch shots, but he kept to par nevertheless and at the end of it all was five under. Only one other competitor, Joe Kirkwood, beat par that day. (As an aside, Jones's 68 was worth about a 63 on the St Andrews of today, played with modern golf equipment.)

Jones again began with less than mechanical perfection the next day and hit two more bad pitches early on, reaching the turn in 37. He then came back in 35, playing more or less perfect golf, but was, however, only two strokes ahead of Bert Hodson, four on Kirkwood and six on Cotton.

A slim lead you would think, yet no less an observer than

Bernard Darwin could write that Jones was already the winner unless 'he bombards continuously the stationmaster's garden'.

On the last day Jones again went out poorly; this time it was 38, which Darwin said usually meant a round of about 77, as the second half of St Andrews was the more testing. Jones again came back in 35.

With a round to go, this was the position:

213   Jones
218   Fred Robson (after a third-round 69)
219   Aubrey Boomer and Joe Kirkwood

Jones could now more definitely afford a drive or two into the stationmaster's garden. Again, he played – it almost seems by force of habit – a poor outward half, pitching into bunkers. On the 9th tee he needed a 4 to be out in 38 but birdied the hole as the first of a sequence of four 3s. The rest was a triumphal progress.

When he reached the Valley of Sin at the front of the last green, it is reliably estimated that there was a crowd of 15,000 to see him finish. He did so nearly to perfection, when a huge putt seemed to have the right pace and line all the way up to the hole. It just grazed past and Jones tapped the resulting 6in one away for a 72.

He had finished six strokes better than Aubrey Boomer and Fred Robson. His winning total of 285 was lower by six shots than the winning score in any previous British Open and was lower than any previous Open score at St Andrews by no less than eleven strokes.

It began a kind of love affair between Bobby Jones and St Andrews. As he left the 18th green all that could be seen of him was his treasured putter, Calamity Jane, a sort of Excalibur of golf and easily the most famous single club in golf history. The club was visible because Jones was holding it high above his head to keep it safe from the multitude – he lost his cap but he did not mind that.

At the presentation that followed, Jones, who was in fact a St Andrews club member, said that he would like to leave the championship trophy in the keeping of the Royal and Ancient for the year – a gesture that increased the affection that was felt for him.

He came back, as far as I know, twice more. In 1936 he was having a European touring holiday and found himself in the area. A game at St Andrews was suggested and the news spread very fast indeed. When he got there he found, to his horror, 2,000 gathered to watch him go round. The horror came from the fact that he had been playing little and badly, but the legend was not to be spoilt. This time he did not go out rather poorly by his own standards. After ten holes he had used only 32 strokes and then parred the 11th. Lack of practice then found him out to some extent and he finished in 72. Nevertheless, it was his play for the first eleven that lived on in memory and became a part of the Jones legend.

There now remained only the wedding to cement the love affair for good. On 9 October 1958 Jones was presented with the Freedom of the City, Benjamin Franklin being the only other American to be thus honoured.

What was it in Jones that inspired both affection and veneration? Paul Gallico, for instance, learnt his writing trade as a sports journalist with a wide-ranging brief. When he gave it up to concentrate on novels, he wrote a book called *Farewell to Sport* which contains a long piece entitled 'One Hero'. The hero is Bobby Jones. Gallico felt that of all the tennis players, boxers, golfers, baseball players, athletes and the rest that he had come to know well in the course of work, Jones was the only one of real stature, without feet of clay, indeed without fault. In the words Chaucer wrote some four hundred years earlier, of all sportsmen Bobby Jones was 'the parfait gentil knight'.

Splendour in a cow pasture – the 1970 US Open

The players were not happy with the Hazeltine National course at Chaska, Minnesota. That fact was the key to the winning and the losing of the 1970 US Open. For a start Hazeltine, at 7,151yd, was the second longest course ever used in this championship,

and as an inland course that had had plenty of rain – some 3in –
it was playing its full length. Normally most professionals look
on a par 5 as a clear birdie chance, requiring at most two woods
to the green. But at Hazeltine those par 5s were out of reach.
This alone made a par round of 72 far more difficult to achieve.

Then there was another problem the players were not used to.
The landscape at Hazeltine was undulating and targets were
often not visible from the tee and sometimes not for the second
shot either. In all, there were eleven holes at which the green was
invisible from the tee, and the use of elevated greens by architect
Robert Trent Jones meant that the flag was partially hidden at
ten holes for the second or third shot. This posed an additional
problem in that the greens themselves were particularly large,
on occasion 40yd in length, so that it was not possible for a
player to have a precise feel of the pin position as he went into
his shot.

Nicklaus summed up opinion when he said that the course
was as difficult as any used for an Open. Dave Hill, one of the
most successful competitors on the US tour that year, went a
little further. He said, 'All it needs is eighty acres of corn and
some cows,' and further defined it as a 'pasture with flags'. The
locals were proud of the cattle and wheat plains of their native
state but did not relish this description of their course. They
mooed at Hill as he made his way along the fairways during the
championship. Hill himself was fined $150 for his remarks, which
he found a fair charge for the pleasure of voicing his feelings.

But many of the entry were even less happy than Hill after the
first round was completed on 18 June 1970. Anyone with a
round as good as a 75 was content, able to feel that he had
mastered the blustering 30–40mph north-westerly wind. But
few did as well as this. Only 81 of the 150 qualifiers were under
80. The 'big three', Palmer, Player and Nicklaus, took 79, 80
and 81 shots respectively. Even Trevino, with the reputation of
being the best wind player in the world, could manage no
better than 77.

For most players throughout the world, golf is a game played
in a shirt and perhaps a light pullover if there is a slight nip in the

air. It is a game played in the humidity of Singapore, the dry heat of South Africa and indeed every variation of warm climate you care to think of, but if there is a winter season it is usual for courses to close down during it. A Swiss course may be open for a few months of the year only and there is a lengthy closed season for much of the US – a reason for the US Tour 'following the sun'. Only in Britain does a high proportion of golfers feel that golf is a game for wind, rain, frost, hail and snow – if it is not too deep, you can paint a few balls orange and carry on!

In these circumstances, it was not surprising that the holder of the British Open, Tony Jacklin, was the one player to beat par, which he did by one shot. He started 3, 5, 5, 2, 3, 3, three under par, and had one other birdie during the first nine holes. (The first threeball were 14 over par on the first four holes!) In the second half he had only one more birdie but throughout kept at bay all but one of the double bogeys that were plaguing so many of the field. Jacklin is a good front runner and not afraid of winning. His temperamental fault rather is to become disinterested if he feels he has lost the chance of winning, when perseverance can often mean that opportunities to capitalise on the falterings of others will present themselves.

Despite his two-stroke lead on Julius Boros and four shots on the nearest other competitor, Jacklin was still nobody's favourite for the championship. Although he had won a tournament in the US and was British Open Champion, first-round leaders seldom win and the weather was now relatively calm. Even those who had started with 80s by no means felt out of contention, because of the freak weather of the previous day. They would throw everything to chance to make up lost ground. Such a player as Nicklaus is often at his psychological best when freed of an inborn conservatism, an unwillingness to take risks, a tendency to aim for the centre of the green rather than at a flag menaced by bunker and water hazard. Surely the 65s and 66s would now become fairly commonplace, despite the length of the course.

At the end of the day Jacklin was the halfway leader. Only

Dave Hill, with 69, had made up ground on him, and then by only one stroke. None of the high scorers of the first round had forced himself up the field. Hazeltine National, and the testing course architecture of R. T. Jones, was winning the battle, for apart from its length there were other menacing features of the course. It is heavily bunkered – more than 100 in all – and very many of them are out of sight as the player makes his shot. Most of the par 4s and 5s are dog-legs, demanding a drive both long and accurate if the player is to have a clear shot to the green for his second. And as Nicklaus put it, there were no 'position Bs' at Hazeltine. An off-line iron or wood from the tee usually meant a shot dropped – unless the player could make up for his error with a chip-and-putt finish. Most of the players disliked the greens and few were getting down in a single putt from more than 4 or 5ft. The putting surfaces were dense and wet, and the ball had to be rapped firmly and confidently over them, but many had lost confidence on that first day – strong winds can be said to affect putting more adversely than they do the longer shots. Nevertheless, Jacklin was averaging only 28 putts per round at that point.

During the third round he maintained his momentum. His putting was slightly less effective but his swing was now perfectly poised and rhythmic and he was perhaps playing in that kind of trance experienced by those at a peak of form. If he made an error, he made up for it with a precise floating wedge to the green, a good chip or a fine putt. He was not, as I have said, afraid of leading, and when in trouble, like Palmer, would be driven by temperament to a bold, sometimes rash or desperate, counter blow. One moment of crisis came on the 344yd 17th when his 2-iron from the tee finished behind trees. He considered merely playing out towards the green, for the trees were really too near and too high for him to get both the height to clear them and the length to reach the green. He slected an 8-iron as likely to give him enough height and lashed into the shot. Up and over it went and on and on for 160yd before settling about 25ft from the hole. Without further alarms he finished the round and signed for a 70. Hill had fallen a shot further behind, firmly in second place but still four shots behind Jacklin. The remainder were seven (Brewer), eight, nine, eleven and worse behind. Gay Brewer had drawn to within two strokes of the leader halfway through the round but his challenge had faded over the second nine holes.

Many tournament players see the third round as being particularly crucial; it is then that a leader must consolidate a good opening. If he does so, it is up to the others to take risks in the final round while he can play the 'safe' shots – play short of a water hazard or line of bunkers, aim for the middle of the green, putt to be sure of getting down in two rather than go boldly at a downhill putt.

Jacklin could not yet disregard Dave Hill, but the course would probably protect him against the 63s and 64s that any other challenger would still need if Jacklin should stumble to over par for his final round. The trouncing of the field that Jacklin had in his grasp was only once threatened. He was one under par for the first six but dropped shots at both of the next two holes. Thoughts of Palmer losing no less than seven strokes to Billy Casper in the 1966 Open always recur in the minds of championship leaders at times like this. At the 9th he was in the rough from the tee but managed to get his 4-iron on to the green about 10yd from the hole. Now to get safely down in two. But his putt was too bold, at least 5 or 6ft too strong, although dead straight. It hit the back of the hole, jumped up in the air and disappeared from sight.

The rest was a triumphal progress. Jacklin stood on the 18th tee with a six-shot lead. He drove safely down the fairway, put a 4-iron on to the green and holed a long putt.

This is how they finished:

281 Tony Jacklin (71, 70, 70, 70)
288 Dave Hill (75, 69, 71, 73)
289 Bob Charles (76, 71, 75, 67)
289 Bob Lunn (77, 72, 70, 70)
291 Ken Still (78, 71, 71, 71)
292 Miller Barber (75, 75, 72, 70)

Page 33 Great swings: *(top left)* Ted Ray, 1910; *(top right)* Francis Ouimet 1923; *(below left)* Bobby Jones, 1926; *(below right)* Gene Sarazen, 1936

Page 34 (above) Three generations: *(left to right)* Henry Cotton, Archie Compston, James Braid, J. H. Taylor, an exhibition game in 1940; *(below left)* Henry Cotton, 1938; *(below right)* great character, great player, Walter Hagen *(plus-fours)* and Archie Compston, 1929

Jacklin had broken no records in winning this championship but he had joined a number of select companies. The only foreigners to win the US Open are Harry Vardon (1900), Ted Ray (1920) and Gary Player (1965). Jacklin's winning margin of seven shots was not the highest on record – Jim Barnes finished nine shots ahead 49 years earlier – and others had led throughout, but not many – only Walter Hagen, Jim Barnes and Ben Hogan. Bobby Jones (twice), Gene Sarazen, Ben Hogan and Jack Nicklaus have also held both the British and US Open Championships at the same time (although only Jones, Sarazen and Hogan have won both in the *same* year).

All of Jacklin's rounds except the first had been a 70. It is interesting that but four players recorded a single round better than this. There were three 69s and a 67 from Bob Charles, who came home strongly with the best round of the tournament. It was, of course, the consistency of his scoring that brought Jacklin home; all his rounds were below par – an achievement he shares with Lee Trevino in the US Open records.

Jacklin returned to England a national hero to defend his British Open title three weeks later. He might have succeeded. On the first round he went out in 29 and was maintaining a momentum towards something between a 62 and a 64 when the weather broke. When he completed the round the next morning the mood was gone.

For Tony Jacklin at Hazeltine in 1970 the future seemed to hold a secure place with the 'big three'. His performance there was one of the supreme achievements in golf history, but since then he has barely held his position as the best British golfer – not enough really in a country that does not often have more than one golfer of the highest world class, and Jacklin today has slipped below this level. If he has the appetite, there is still time.

Better than Nicklaus? - the 1974 British Open

Those who know what golf is all about laughed when they first saw Gary Player swing. His grip was all wrong, his swing flat, and he nearly came off his feet with the effort he put into the long shots in the attempt to keep up with men of bigger physique. When he joined the British tour in the early 1950s, little was predicted for him; he sometimes found it difficult even to get leading British professionals of the day to allow him to play with them during practice rounds. Perhaps it was the intensity of the man, the burning keenness to learn, that alienated them from him. If you wanted to win in Britain, you should not let it show too much; to come third with charm could make you more highly valued than to win while showing that you cared about the outcome of a tournament more than was quite gentlemanly.

Player learned, trained, practised. Indeed his morning press-ups, weight-training, running and long hours on the practice grounds, once he had established himself as a winner, made him a symbol of what you could do if you really tried, even if your natural ability was less than that of many others.

His first entry in a British Open came in 1955; his first victory in 1959. He won it again in 1968 at Carnoustie, then perhaps the toughest course that has been presented to a championship field at any time, anywhere. In between, he had added the US Open, US PGA and the Masters to his major-championship record, had won a host of other tournaments approaching the hundred mark, and had shown himself to be the best matchplay golfer in the world by making the Piccadilly World Matchplay Championship very nearly his personal property.

But Gary Player had set out wanting to be the best golfer in the world; it rankled with him that few would concede him this status. Palmer at his peak was thought his superior, and then Jack Nicklaus came along. By 1973 there were the sub-par surges of Johnny Miller and the superb striking of Tom Weiskopf. In the 1960s the 'big three' had been Palmer, Nicklaus and Player; as 1974 began it seemed that the 'big three' were now Weiskopf, Miller and Nicklaus.

Palmer's days, at least in retrospect, were long over. Instead of the last-round charges that had made him famous, he tended to fade away in the final round. Player was also nearing the end of the road as a serious contender in major championships, it seemed. He had been at the top just about longer than anyone, and you can measure a golfer's age not by years alone but possibly more by the period of time he has spent as a major golfer; by the wear and tear of holing 3ft putts, keeping it straight from the tee, hitting iron shots of flawless precision at the flag.

After two rounds at Augusta National in April, Gary Player, after a pair of 71s, lay behind almost everyone who was eventually to finish in the top dozen and he was five behind the leader, Dave Stockton. The prescient Henry Longhurst wrote that Player's great days were almost certainly behind him. The next day, he went round in 66 and a day later was donning the celebrated green jacket of the Master's champion for a second time, winner by two strokes over Stockton and Tom Weiskopf.

He followed with further successes on the US circuit, but when he arrived at Royal Lytham and St Annes for the British Open he had not quite displaced Nicklaus as the automatic favourite. A first-round 69 to Nicklaus's 74 changed all that, and Player led the field, equalled only by a man called John Morgan, who caused many to retell the story of how, en route to a 92 in the 1968 Carnoustie Open, he had been bitten by a rat in the rough.

Lytham was a fine test of golf in strong winds, with the luck of the bounce to contend with on fairways and greens that tended to hold only those shots that had been truly struck.

In similar conditions the next day, Player went one better and was in the sole lead by five strokes – the largest gap at this stage of an Open since Henry Cotton had put the field to the sword at Sandwich in 1934 by starting off 67, 65.

It always used to be said that the third round is the crucial one. Can a leader maintain the momentum he has built up, or will he begin too soon to play defensively in the effort to preserve what he has already achieved? Or will someone lying well back suddenly find that the putts are dropping? It appeared unlikely, for Player had been showing better than anyone how control over a variety of shots is needed when the winds blow. Making full use of his 1-iron, which he later said he loved equally with his wife, he had kept the ball low into the wind and varied the shape of his shots according to the wind direction. In this area of technique, he had come to rank with Peter Thomson as a master of linksland golf in wind. (It was interesting to contrast Thomson and Miller at one of the short holes with a strong, left-to-right wind blowing. Miller took something like a 6-iron, aimed a little left of the pin and let fly a high shot which came in towards the flag and then continued to do so until he was nearly out of bounds to the right of the green. Thomson, on the other hand, took a much straighter-faced club and hit it left of the green almost directly into the wind. The gentle curve of his ball through the air as it faded to the flag was far different from the almost violent swing of Miller's as the wind had grasped it and flung it away.)

However, in the third round Player faded a little. His 75 allowed Peter Oosterhuis to gain two shots on him, while Jack Nicklaus's 70 pulled him to within four shots of the South African. Many others had faltered too. A young American, Danny Edwards, had gone to 76, after 70, 73, as had Bobby Cole and Lu Liang-Huan. Only Oosterhuis, Nicklaus and Hubert Green (71, 74, 71) could, with realism, have felt they had any sort of chance of catching Player, and then only if he weakened again.

Player seemed to put the doubts of his 75, during which the greatest of bunker artists had topped an attempted recovery into the face, immediately behind him. At the 206yd 1st he brought a 5-iron in off a bank towards the hole and sank his putt for a 2. At the 436yd 2nd he took his 1-iron from the tee and then hit his second shot to 4ft, and again the putt went down. After that it was not likely that anyone would catch him, particularly as Oosterhuis, his playing partner, had three-putted the 1st. However, he gained a shot on Player at the 3rd when he rolled in a putt that was every bit of 10yd and must have been further encouraged when Player bunkered his second to the 393yd 4th and failed to make his par.

At the 212yd 5th both failed to make par, and on the course the position was that Player lay four ahead of Oosterhuis and Nicklaus and five ahead of Green, Weiskopf and 'Mr Lu', who had played the first seven holes with four pars and three birdies.

Many of Player's championship wins have been distinguished by particularly telling shots into the flag, and he produced just such a one at the 486yd, par-5 6th – a long iron that came to rest a couple of yards or so from the flag. That was an eagle, and though the 7th, 551yd, was out of range in two for him, he produced a well-judged pitch and a birdie 4 was the result. He was now five shots ahead of Oosterhuis and Nicklaus, who was taking two putts per green and therefore making no advance.

It was almost all over – but that has been said many times before. Player still had to keep it going; Nicklaus might begin at last to putt to the same standard as his play through the green and Peter Oosterhuis, as good as anyone in the world at short pitching, chipping, and putting, was buoyed by the support of a British crowd.

On the 11th Nicklaus did get one in for a birdie, but then missed from 5ft at the 13th and knew that, for him, it was over. He dropped further strokes at each of the three following par 4s.

For the elusive target of the 201yd 12th Player again took out the 1-iron and his shot flew like a bullet at the green. But the final holes were still not to be without drama. At the next Player holed an 8-iron chip for a birdie and his lead seemed decisive. On the 15th he dropped a shot and then, at the 17th, he pulled a 6-iron into deep rough that Player called 'the thickest I have ever seen so close to a green in twenty years of championship golf'. Many saw exactly where his ball had gone and at least a dozen, with Player the most energetic among them, scrambled for it.

Had Oosterhuis still a chance? If Player had to go back and play what would have been his fourth shot from the fairway, and if he were then again to miss the green, and if Oosterhuis could . . . But the ball was found deep down in the damp heavy grass. Player was able to move it only a handful of yards but this was enough. He chipped carefully and dropped the one stroke only.

There was still a minor alarm left for him. His second to the 386yd final hole skipped through the green and came to rest almost hard against the clubhouse wall. Player had to putt it back left-handed. Having a five-stroke lead, he did not appear unduly disturbed and looked fully competent standing the 'wrong way round'.

Player, 282; Oosterhuis, 286; Nicklaus, 287; Green, 288; four more shots till we get to the next man. The new champion's winning margin had been bettered only three times since the championship began again after World War II, and only Harry Vardon had previously won the Open in three different decades. One of the measures of a great golfer is surely how long he remains great, and in this Player can stand comparison with anybody.

For the first time in years another comparison was being made. Player now had eight major championship wins to Nicklaus's twelve and was suddenly within reach of the achievements of not only Nicklaus, but also of Bobby Jones in the 1920s and his Grand Slam year, 1930.

Characteristically Player felt the comparisons were being made on the wrong terms. 'What about my Piccadilly World Matchplay Championships and the South African and Australian Opens?' he asked. What indeed. The record then begins to flatter Player and do Nicklaus no good at all.

	Player	Nicklaus
Piccadilly	5	1
South African Open	8	0
Australian Open	7	4

So we now have Nicklaus with eighteen wins to the end of 1975 and Player with a total of twenty-eight! However, the South African Open really cannot be admitted to the list: it by no means draws a majority of the best golfers. The Piccadilly field, with only eight competitors invited, is too limited; three good rounds and you are the winner. The Australian Open, however, gives Player a better case to argue. All the best Australians compete and there is usually a respectable sprinkling of entrants from overseas. Winners over the last twenty years include Bobby Locke, Bruce Crampton, Kel Nagle, Bruce Devlin, Arnold Palmer, Peter Thomson, Jack Nicklaus and, frequently, Gary Player.

I think, however, that if you asked any of the best golfers which were the most *difficult* tournaments to win, the answer would come: the Open, the US Open/Masters and the US PGA. Perhaps Player should rest his case on his performances in the British Open – he has won that three times to Nicklaus's two!

All on the Last Round

Arrivals and a departure – the 1960 US Open

WALTER HAGEN said that no one remembers who came second, a remark that is often quoted in agreement. I am not sure he was entirely right. For instance, in the 1939 US Open Sam Snead (though no one told him) needed just a 6 on the last hole to qualify for a play-off. In going for perilous recovery shots he finished with an 8. It was Snead's best US Open; he must have played in more than thirty since and has never won it. The winner? Byron Nelson, his victory less remembered than Snead's defeat.

In the case of the 1960 US Open the winner's name has certainly survived – Arnold Palmer. He just managed to squeeze in for what seemed likely to be the first of several wins. In fact, though he later was to come close eight or nine times, the 1960 tournament remains his solitary victory, but as a result there is no question mark against his name as there is against Sam Snead's. Perhaps Snead has won a different kind of recognition. No one else approaches his record of being right at the top, or very near the top, for a full forty years. Finishing third in the 1974 PGA is still pretty near.

But to me the 1960 US Open at Denver, Colorado, is much more than the story of Palmer's last-round race to victory. It is also Hogan's last chance; Jack Nicklaus making his first bid; the story of what happened to poor Mike Souchak; how Jack Fleck might have done it again and thereby not gone down into golf history as the man who happened to take the Open from Ben Hogan in 1955.

It was all Souchak for the first two rounds, which he completed in 68, 67, taking only 26 putts in that first 68 and not many more in the next round. He kept on going from that base until

45

his last shot through the green on the last hole of the third round. Then he hooked into a pond and eventually dropped two strokes on the hole – 73. Instead of being almost as far ahead as Henry Cotton had been in the 1934 British Open, Souchak had given his pursuers cause for hope. In fact, as the final round developed, at least eight players were in contention by the halfway stage.

The round opened with Souchak on 208 (68, 67, 73), followed by two; players on 211 Hogan (75, 67, 69) and the twenty-year-old Jack Nicklaus (71, 71, 69), who was playing, he has said, as well then as at any time since, feeling in an ideal hitting position for all his shots.

For Palmer the round opened with a deficit of seven shots and an idea. The idea concerned the 1st hole. Though it was a par 4, drives travelled further in the rarified hill air of the Cherry Hills course in Denver and the green could be reached by the longest hitters, of which Palmer was one. But there was rough shielding the final approaches to the green and other hazards paralleled the fairway: a ditch on one side, poplars and pines the other. Most of the golfers throughout the tournament had played safe by taking an iron from the tee to keep clear of the trouble to either side and also to ensure they would not reach the rough before the green. After the iron shot they had only a short approach shot left anyway, so they still had a good chance of a birdie.

Palmer had been after the certain birdie and possible eagle that getting a drive through the guarding rough and on to the green would bring. As he began his final round, his driver at this hole had only brought him the sequence 6, 5, 4, whereas few others were worse than level 4s on it for the tournament. Never mind, Palmer was difficult to disconcert once there was an attacking, daring stroke to be played. Again he took out his driver. This time his ball did not drift into ditch or pine forest but skidded through the rough and lay clear on the putting surface.

Palmer did not, in fairy-tale style, get his eagle 2 but two putts and a birdie were enough to set him off on a memorable burst of scoring. At the 410yd 2nd he boosted his hopes further by chipping in, followed with a 3 on the 348yd 3rd and then holed a huge putt of about 15yd on the 4th. Four holes played; four birdies. In theory he might now be only three strokes behind Souchak. He parred the 5th, had birdies on each of the next two holes and then went on to complete the outward half in 30, a scoring record for the US Open. But like Miller in the same event thirteen years later, he had started far behind the leaders and had caught but not passed most of them. But by the 10th he was level with Souchak, and two holes later he had pulled ahead.

One of the most difficult things to do in golf is to come back once a commanding lead has been surrendered. Souchak, like many others before and after him, did not succeed in doing so. In his last round he faded away to a 75 and total of 283. So from this point on the championship was fought out amongst a formidable company who were all tied for the lead at some time after the first half: Ben Hogan, Jack Fleck, Jack Nicklaus, Dutch Harrison, Ted Kroll, Julius Boros and Dow Finsterwald.

Fleck's dramatic tie with Hogan in 1955 and his even more unexpected victory in the eighteen holes play-off the next day had not brought him fortune and only a temporary fame. An American must win the US Open to reach the golfer's Hall of Fame, but he must then go on to do more. Fleck had done relatively little else since he had played entranced at Olympic five years before. But if he were to win *another* Open, it would be a far different matter.

He began his chase for the title every bit as dramatically as Palmer. He too had five birdies at the first six holes and the leaders, who mostly were playing ahead of him, had someone else to think about. Especially Ben Hogan who must have wondered if Fleck was again to be his Nemesis, again to prevent his winning the US Open for a record fifth time.

The forty-eight-year-old Hogan was paired with Nicklaus for the final two rounds and Hogan was giving a supreme demonstration of his mastery of manoeuvring a golf ball from tee to green. In his third round 69 he had hit the green in the regulation number of strokes every time but had holed few birdie putts.

Some great golfers have begun as good putters and have rapidly become anything from nervous to locked rigid in fright when standing over a short putt. In some cases it has seemed that the more masterful a player is with his long shots – and even approach putts – the less sure he becomes once his ball is a mere stride from the hole. Harry Vardon, for example, became incapable of producing anything resembling a smooth stroke at the ball; Snead looked rather better but the ball all too frequently did not go into the hole until he tried a between-the-legs croquet style – and that was quickly banned by the rulers of golf. There is even a story about one US Open Champion who refused to putt in exhibition games. He would play his shots to the green and once there impassively pick up his ball. Spectators thought that he felt the humdrum business of getting the ball into the hole was too simple a matter to be worthy of a great golfer's attention. The reality was that he did not want the news to get out that he was likely to average four putts a green and sometimes jerk the ball clean off it in a nerve spasm.

Hogan had been one of the great putters, in the Hagen, Jones and Palmer class, but it had gone. In middle age you would see him practise an ingenious variety of putting strokes before addressing the ball. None of them resembled the tortured action with which, eventually, he prodded it towards the hole – after freezing over the ball for an eternity. How is it that a man like Hogan or Vardon can place a ball *there* or *there* with his tee shot and long irons into the green yet be inferior to many middle-handicap golfers once he takes putter in hand? Perhaps the answer lies in the fact that a golfer is dealing with two elements – air and earth (not water as well, that's just something he picks out of for a one-stroke penalty). He can master the flight of a ball through the air. If there has been perfection of swing and judgement of wind effect, distance and perhaps even atmospheric density, the ball will fly with the trajectory and velocity his clubhead has given it. But eventually it has to come to ground and is then prey to the malignity of another element – earth. The golfer learns to accept that his ball may pitch on a slightly soft centimetre of turf and stop more quickly than he had anticipated, or land on another spot and perhaps unkindly bound on through the green. Often, indeed, fate can be with him and a shot struck too weakly may fortunately run on to the flag. But on the putting green few golfers will admit that a putt they have struck was lucky to dive into the hole, perhaps after being minutely diverted by a spike mark. Very readily, however, they will complain of the 'something' that made their ball stop short of the hole, twist off the edge or divert from the true line they have struck it along.

Over the passage of the years the number of blows from a harsh fate met while putting mount up in the mind of a golfer of excellence. In the end he knows, every time he putts, that some disaster lies immediately ahead. His pessimism then reaches the same level as Vardon's and Hogan's. He delays the time when he will just *have* to hit the ball by lengthily examining the line and practising his stroke before standing statuesque over the ball, and eventually he hits it with no better effect than if he had strolled up to his ball and tapped it at the hole on the walk (a remedy that has often been tried).

On that last afternoon of the 1960 US Open, however, Hogan at last began to make some putts, and there was the spectacle of youth and age, Nicklaus and Hogan, both in close pursuit of the title. For the former it would have been a glittering prize at the outset of what seemed set fair to be a great career. Nicklaus would have earned comparison with Bobby Jones as the greatest amateur of his era and the first since Johnny Goodman in 1933 (not a vintage year) to win it. For Hogan, victory would have been the fitting and well-earned final peak of a life's work devoted to striking a golf ball with ultimate purity.

Nicklaus eagled the par-5 5th and eventually turned in 32. If he could maintain this kind of scoring Palmer would not catch him with anything worse than a 60. Nicklaus then faltered slightly, dropping a stroke to par on the 11th, which, as a par 5, he would have hoped to birdie. Hogan continued in his by now set pattern of hitting every green in the regulation figures and then getting down in two putts – but not the single putts he needed to master the field.

At the 212yd 12th Hogan took a wood and hit in a shot to 10ft. At last he holed the putt. Nicklaus also holed for a 2 and this put him a stroke up on Palmer, Boros and Fleck. At the 385yd 13th Hogan safely got his par but Nicklaus did not. He had pitched up to about 12ft but three-putted and then did so once more on the next, a 470yd par 4. Mechanically, Hogan again had a par. At the 15th, a par 3, he drew level with the leaders, who at this point on the course were Arnold Palmer and Jack Fleck, at four under par for the championship. Hogan had single-putted from all of 6 or 7yd; was the worst element in his game, putting, about to take the championship for him? He had hit thirty-two consecutive greens and was now getting the putts into the hole.

At the 16th both Nicklaus and Hogan had chances for birdies, but both failed to get their putts down. They now faced perhaps the most dangerous hole on the course. The 17th measured 548yd. This would normally mean that Nicklaus would have no difficulty in making the distance in two strokes, while Hogan could also expect to if he could put together two outstanding wooden-club shots. But the second shot at the 17th was perilous in the extreme, for the green was set on an island in a lake. The second shot could not, therefore, merely bounce and run on to the green; it had to pitch on and stop quickly, so the player needed to be using an iron for his second, and a very straight iron at that. Both decided not to hazard the championship on the one shot and played to a few yards of the lake. They would try to lay their short pitches close to the hole. Nicklaus went 3 or 4yd past the hole, having played a safe shot that was never in danger of finding the water.

Hogan pondered his shot. He could play the simple shot that would run at least a few yards past the flag or he could hazard hitting a sand wedge at the flag, which was positioned well to the front of the green, and risk spinning back into the water. He took his sand wedge, opened the face and hit a low shot with all the backspin he could work on to the ball. It cleared the lake, pitched, and spun back into the shallows at the edge. Although he played a good shot from the water it was a 6, not the 4 that would have left him needing a 4 at the last for 279 and, in probability, his fifth US Open. With that shot which he had

Page 51 Putting pressures: *(right)* Lee Trevino, Muirfield 1972, *(below)* Roberto de Vicenzo, Troon 1973

Page 52 Putting concentration: *(left)* Johnny Miller, Troon 1973; *(below)* Peter Oosterhuis, 1974

played almost too well Hogan was finished, almost an old man as the competitive fire drained out of him. While Nicklaus went one over par on the last to finish with a 5, Hogan finished with an exhausted 7.

The rest was Arnold Palmer, playing about two holes behind Hogan and Nicklaus. After his burst of low-scoring on the outward half, he needed, as it turned out, only to par his way in if the others continued to drop shots – they all did.

After he had holed his final short putt, there was a pause of about half an hour and then Palmer was champion.

This is how they finished:

280   Arnold Palmer (72, 71, 72, 65)
282   Jack Nicklaus (71, 71, 69, 71)
283   Dutch Harrison, Julius Boros, Ted Kroll, Dow Finster-
      wald, Mike Souchak (68, 67, 73, 75) and Jack Fleck
284   Ben Hogan (75, 67, 69, 73)

The greatest round of all? – the 1973 US Open

Oakmont is one of the greatest of US courses, and since its foundation its custodians have been zealous to see that par is not mocked. In the 1935 Open, for example, only the winner brought in a total below 300 and even then this was by a scant single shot.

At that time there were several reasons. The course was very heavily bunkered – some individual ones could almost be measured in acres – and the bunkers were raked into deep furrows. This meant that, whatever the quality of the player, if trapped in a bunker flanking a fairway he could do no more than blast his ball out – there was only a remotest chance of taking a shot clean and hitting on to a green 150–200yd away. More important, however, was the condition of the greens. Oakmont was designed with traditional British courses in mind. The greens were hard and kept cut to about $\frac{3}{32}$in for championship play. This meant that a shot pitched at the flag was far more likely to run well through than not. A player had to study just exactly where he ought to land his ball to have it run on towards the flag. The antithesis of 'target' golf in fact. So winners had to be able to play every iron in the bag and be capable of varying the kind of shot played with particular clubs.

By 1973 some of this had changed. Bunker raking, for instance, was by no means as penal. Furrowing was not as deep and this meant that superb shots from the bunkers towards distant greens were possible (perhaps more fair as all were no longer reduced to the same level of having to play the simple explosion shot out on to the fairway). But the greens had not changed. As at Augusta National they remained fearsomely fast and the demands made by the hard approaches were much the same as they had been decades before. One noted player, Dave Hill, withdrew before the championship began, feeling that his techniques were inadequate to deal with the problems.

In the May of 1973, however, it had rained for many days of the month. When the championship began, Oakmont was not quite as fast and hard a course as it usually was. Nevertheless its greens were still quick. In the first round the negro Charlie Sifford had begun badly but at least he was on the par-4 7th in two and looking for a birdie. Some time later he holed a putt of around an inch for an 8. And he seemed to have been trying on the first four attempts.

Player managed the greens best of all. Always given to extremes when talking about his game, he said that he could not possibly have putted better, that he felt that he had played one of the rounds of his life. In fact, after a 67, he led the field by three clear shots, followed by Lee Trevino and Jim Colbert on 70 and Nicklaus, Miller, Littler, Palmer, Charles and Johnston with 71.

There is much dispute about what happened that night, but all are agreed that the greens were watered. It was supposed to be for five minutes only, but defects in the sprinkler system were alleged and in some cases the period may have been very much longer.

For the second round Oakmont was a different course. Dave Hill's replacement, a club pro called Gene Borek, went round in

65, which was but one stroke above the US Open Championship record. The day before he had taken 77. However, no one else humbled the course to this extent and at the end of the day the situation amongst those with a winning chance had altered very little.

The favourites were Nicklaus – as usual – who had won four tournaments that year, and Weiskopf, who had suddenly reached his full potential and had finished first, second, first and first in the last four tournaments he had played. Nicklaus lay joint third on 140 and Weiskopf had improved to a 69 after an opening 73. Player still led on 137 but by a shot only now. Colbert was still second, and on 140 with Jack Nicklaus were Bob Charles and Johnny Miller.

That night it rained heavily. The next day, playing an approach to the green was as much a target golf shot as any other, but even this did not seem to suit everyone. Miller took 76 and seemed to have put himself out of serious contention – you do not win the US Open or anything else if you take 76. Nicklaus took 74. Others, however, found the conditions more to their liking.

Jerry Heard had a 66 to lead jointly on 210 with fifty-three-year-old Julius Boros (73, 69, 68), John Schlee (73, 70, 67) and Arnold Palmer (71, 71, 68). Weiskopf had had another 69 and followed on 211. Trevino, Charles and Colbert were one shot behind him and then followed Player on 214, after a disastrous 77, Littler 215 and Miller and others on 216.

As the final round opened the questions were: could Palmer at last win another major title? Was Boros too old to win the Open a third time? Would Nicklaus abandon caution and produce his almost customary storming final round?

Of course, no one was asking any questions about Johnny Miller, whose reputation was as a promising rather than as an established player. He had done very well at nineteen to finish 8th in the 1966 Open, had come close to winning the 1971 Masters before dropping too many shots on the finishing holes, and in 1970 had had an astonishing round of 61 in a circuit tournament. So far he had won two tournaments and had played well in Opens, though usually recording a poor final round which left him well down the list.

Going out one hour behind the leaders, he began with four birdies, two of which required only tap-in putts. Suddenly, from being six shots behind the leaders, he was only two behind. He played the next three holes in regulation figures and came to the 8th, one of the most difficult holes on which to make par on the course. This is a 244yd par 3, bounded on the right by a road and on the left by the Sahara bunker, which stretches along the fairway for well over 100yd. Miller, having put his tee shot on the green, then three-putted for his only bogey of the round. At the time, since he could afford to drop nothing, it seemed that his challenge might be over.

The crowds were still following Weiskopf, Boros and, more than anyone, Palmer. The lead alternated amongst them and, after nine holes, each was four under par.

Miller did not falter after the 8th. On the 480yd 9th he put a long iron about 12yd from the hole and down went his putt. He was out in 32. After another par he then birdied the next three holes but on the 14th missed a birdie putt from 9ft. On the 15th tee he was seven under for the round and four under for the tournament. He then hit a 4-iron second shot that came to rest about 9ft short of the hole. He sank the putt for his ninth birdie of the round.

Palmer had just played a second shot to about 4ft at the 11th and had missed the putt. As far as he knew, however, he was still in the lead at four under with Weiskopf and Boros one behind, together with John Schlee, who had been playing well after having a double bogey on the 1st. As Palmer left the 12th tee, after hitting what he thought had been a perfect drive down the left, he saw a scoreboard. It showed that Miller, not Palmer, was leading at five under. And his drive was not perfect – far from it. Instead of following the slope of the ground from left to right, the ball had kicked against it and shot off the fairway. He had hoped to reach the 603yd 12th green in two or at least have a short pitch left for his third; instead, all he could do was get the ball out of the rough with an iron and squirt it some way along the fairway. He still had a full wood-shot left. He put that into the rough and then pitched too far past the hole and took 6. That was the end of his attempt on the 1973 Open, for he then bogeyed the next two holes.

Miller had at least to hold what he had, not let the shots slip as he had done the only other time he had been near winning a major championship. He got his par 3 at the 230yd 16th and then came to the 322yd par-4 17th. This was a hole whose length alone gave a clear birdie opportunity. There were two routes to the green. If you could carry the ball 270yd over a copse you might well finish on the green – Nicklaus adopted that strategy. Miller did not, but still had a 9ft putt for a birdie after a wedge shot. It did not drop.

The last hole at Oakmont is one of the most difficult par 4s there, or anywhere else. It measures 465yd and a powerful drive is needed. Miller hit one a whisker under 300yd and had only a medium iron left for his shot to the green. That finished some 6yd from the hole. His putt hit the hole but stayed out. That made him round in 63.

But Miller, back in the clubhouse, had still not won. Palmer was gone beyond hope of repair, but John Schlee had to get birdies on two of the last three holes to tie. He got one on the 16th, parred the 17th and put his approach to the 18th just through the back of the green. His chip to tie failed by a few inches. Weiskopf had to go one better. He too birdied the 16th and then put his second 12ft from the hole at the next. When he narrowly missed, Miller was champion.

There are several candidates to claim the greatest round in the US Open: Palmer with a last-round 65 to win the 1960; Tommy Jacobs's 64 in the second round of the 1964 Open; Ben Hogan's finishing 67 on the monster course of Oakland Hills in 1951; Nicklaus's winning 65 in 1967. Others too have gone as low as 64 – eventually to finish nowhere. But Johnny Miller's round set undisputed records. It is the lowest round ever played in either the US or British Open and it produced the lowest total, 279, to win an Open at Oakmont.

Oakmont, after rain and watering, may not have been the

terror it usually is, but, if we can say that 'anyone' could have shot a low round that day, the fact remains that of those in contention no one else came remotely near Miller's achievement. At the time observers felt that, great round as it was, Miller had done nothing like it before and perhaps never would again. Looking back, we can see that it was the success that took him from the foothills to the sustained plateau he has since been on. It was followed shortly afterwards by his coming close to winning the British Open and then, in the spring of 1975, making rounds in the low 60s seem almost commonplace. In the 1975 Masters he nearly repeated his Oakmont performance when, after opening with 75, 71 to Nicklaus's 68, 67, he chased him home in 65, 66 and had a putt of about 12ft to force a play-off. Perhaps for the rest of the 1970s his chances will not be written off – unless he is just not there any more, having failed to qualify for the final two rounds.

A perfect achievement – the 1953 British Open

No one ever wanted to be the best golfer in the world more than Ben Hogan. For him it was a striving for perfection. Others might want to make a tidy fortune on the US circuit or reap the kudos of being an Open Champion, but for Hogan the ultimate target was to achieve perfection in striking a golf ball.

It took him a long time to do it. In the late 1930s he was a golfer of merit but many others ranked above him, and he neared thirty before he made a real impact. When he returned from war service, confronted by the astonishing run of success of Byron Nelson at that time, he rapidly became fully acknowledged as America's finest as Nelson lost a great deal of his competitive toughness and retired from the tournament circuit. Hogan had been an occasional hooker, with his right hand a touch too far under the shaft and a three-to-four knuckle left-hand grip. He changed his grip and developed even further his anti-hook remedy of a straight-arm thrust through the ball with his right. But, as everyone knows, he was smashed up in a road accident early in 1949 and it was thought that his golf career was finished. Instead, the extra challenge of combating a broken body made him a legend.

He struggled back in 1950 – nearly winning his first tournament, which he finally lost to Sam Snead in a play-off – and by 1953 was playing the finest golf of his life. In that year he took the US Masters and then the US Open. He was urged on to the one achievement still lacking – to win in Britain. He had not proved that he could master the arts of the pitch and run, of playing on a links course, of handling what the British climate might throw at him.

Hogan had been in Britain before as captain of the 1949 US Ryder Cup team but his legs had still not been strong enough to carry him around a golf course. He had listened to advice, from Gene Sarazen in particular, and decided to go to Carnoustie, where the British Open was to be held, forgoing playing in the American PGA.

Thorough as always, Hogan gave himself plenty of time to prepare. By the time the championship opened he knew the course as well as a local club member. Often he played three balls off every tee, seeking the best direction to open up the approach shot to the green, and paced each hole in the reverse direction – from green to tee – to give himself a better grasp of the undulating fairways and the position of hazards. Some of what he saw he did not like, and his remarks caused offence. He described the slow greens, which were not cut short, as 'like putty' and announced he would send to Texas for a lawnmower. He had also to change his striking method for iron shots. On the hard Carnoustie fairways he was jarring his wrists too much as he punched the clubhead into the turf. He began to take the ball more cleanly and soon was playing his irons in just the way that Scottish golfers have done since time immemorial – but better.

He enjoyed using the British ball (0·06 of an inch smaller than the American), finding that with his low, boring flight he could drive it up to 300yd along the links turf. As Carnoustie was over 7,000yd in length he felt that wooden-club play would be crucial and concentrated on that aspect of the game, hoping he could believe assurances that the greens would be cut close for the championship.

When the time came for the two qualifying rounds he was ready, experiencing no problems in finishing comfortably amongst those who would contest the championship proper. It must have been obvious to him, however, that this would be no easy triumph. The defending champion, already a three-times winner, had proved he was in good form by finishing five shots ahead of the rest of the field and nine better than Hogan. Bobby Locke would not give it up easily. Also in the field were the young Australian, Peter Thomson, who would soon win the championship three years running; Frank 'Muscles' Stranahan, the US amateur who practised more than just about any professional; Roberto de Vicenzo and Tony Cerda from South America; several British players with enough ability to win, of whom the best that year was probably the Welshman Dai Rees; and Hogan's fellow American, Lloyd Mangrum, could by no means be ruled out. After taking 78 in the first qualifying round he had come right back with a 67.

The Scottish summer was not kind for the first round: cold, windy and with occasional hail. Probably it is not the difference in type of course that golfers from other countries find their main difficulty but the weather. Golf with comfortably warm hands, light slacks and a thin sports shirt is a different proposition from when the golfer has to add windproof trousers, two pullovers and a rainproof jacket – and still cannot keep warm. Nevertheless, an American led the field at the end of the day but it was Frank Stranahan, not Hogan. Stranahan was on 70, followed by the Scotsman, Eric Brown, on 71, Locke, Thomson, Rees and de Vicenzo, 72 and then Hogan, one stroke further behind. He had looked to have a much better round in hand and was one under par with three holes left. He had finished 4, 5, 5, when 3, 4, 4 was strict par. True, the greens had been cut short, but Hogan still found them too slow and had missed several birdie chances by being short with his putts.

There was no hail the following day and Hogan went to his work with a will. His start promised well – 4, 4, 3, 3, against par of 4, 4, 4, 4. He continued to play well from tee to green but his putting did not convince as he continually played short of the hole. Nevertheless 71 was good enough to put him within two shots of the leaders, Rees and Brown on 142, who were followed by de Vicenzo on 143. Sharing Hogan's mark were Stranahan and Thomson, while the defending champion was 145.

By now Hogan had caught a cold and faced the two rounds of the final day with antibiotics. He did not start off at his best, dropping strokes at the 4th and 5th. Then at the 565yd 6th he lashed two wood shots close to the green and chipped and putted for a birdie. Another followed at the next. He holed a 9ft putt for a birdie 2 on the 168yd 16th and with two holes to go needed a couple of 4s to give him the lead and a 68. But on the next he cut his 4-wood to the green into a bunker, came out weakly and then three-putted, having been short of the hole again with his approach putt. However, he got his expected birdie on the 525yd last hole and, with 214, held the joint lead with Roberto de Vicenzo. Close behind with 215 were Rees, Thomson and Cerda, who had had a 69. Stranahan was on 217 as was Eric Brown, Scotland's main hope, who had faded to a 75. Probably Bobby Locke was now too far behind at 219 to be likely to offer a real threat in the last round.

Hogan began with four 4s and then had his first stroke of luck around the greens. His simple approach at the 389yd 5th kicked off the edge of the green, ran down a slope and came to rest within a hair's breadth of a bunker. For his 10yd chip up to the pin Hogan had an uneven stance – one foot in the bunker. He played the shot well and it hit the back of the hole, popped up in the air, and went down. For the first time Hogan was in front.

He now had some idea what he had to do to win. Cerda was a stroke behind him and de Vicenzo had gone out in 38 – probably too many to give him much hope of winning. Again he birdied the long 6th after two superbly struck woods to the green. Hogan, despite middle age and the fact that he weighed only a little over 9st, was driving the ball as long as anyone in the field, with perhaps the exception of the majestic drawn shots of de Vicenzo.

He continued steadily in par to be out in 34. By now he knew that other contenders had put in totals that would not offer a real threat if he could keep to par on the run in. Rees had played at his best but would have had better than a 71 had he not dropped shots on the 15th and 16th. Stranahan had come back in 32, holing a 14yd putt for an eagle on the last and single-putting on each of the last six greens. This had given him a 69 and the same total as Rees – 286. Hogan would still have to keep an ear open for news of Cerda, playing behind him. Thomson, ahead, might improve on the others but could not win as long as Hogan could keep it up.

Hogan never faltered. He parred each hole on the second nine except for the 168yd 13th, where he had a 2, and the last, where the huge gallery saw him get a birdie 4. His final 68 was a competitive record for the course and gave him a total of 282, four strokes clear of Rees, Stranahan, Thomson and Cerda and another on de Vicenzo, who was to continue to play well in the British Open year after year until he was really too old to win – and then did so.

Hogan left as the only man to win the British Open on his first attempt and did not enter again. He had come and he had conquered.

He returned to America, as a national hero, to a New York ticker-tape welcome. His victory revived the question disputed down the years: who is the greatest golfer the world has seen? Vardon? Jones? Hogan? Nicklaus? Some other candidate? Hogan had really the best answer to that one. He said that all a golfer can do is beat the best in his own day. And he did.

Doing it when it matters – the 1928 British Open

In the spring of 1975 Jimmy Connors of the US faced John Newcombe of Australia in a match for hundreds of thousands of dollars that was also supposed to settle who was the best tennis player in the world. Perhaps its outcome did settle something – but tennis is not golf. In the same period there were proposals for a match between Jack Nicklaus and Johnny Miller for similar amounts of money and with the same aim. Miller had been in a streak of what could be argued as the most sustained spell of low-scoring golf of all time. Nicklaus was the enthroned world Number One, and wanted nothing to do with it. Who wins a golf match proves only that A was better than B on a particular course at a particular time.

For these and many other reasons today's leading golfers fight shy of such encounters. True, they do play individual matches, but in the main they are determined that these should be called 'exhibitions'; there is relatively little advance publicity and the results earn short paragraphs only in the press.

Nevertheless the golfing public is eager for such encounters, as is proved by the demand for tickets at the Piccadilly World Matchplay held at Wentworth every year since 1964. But this involves the gathering together of eight players, a few of whom usually do not rank amongst the world's best eight, and the chances of a Miller and a Nicklaus meeting in the final are slight. Any contest between them is far more likely to be fought out in the context of the US or British Open, the US PGA or the Masters, strokeplay events in which it is the top golfers against the field rather than each other.

This aversion to the big match was not always so. Around the turn of the century they were commonplace in Britain, involving such figures as J. H. Taylor, Harry Vardon, James Braid, Ted Ray and Sandy Herd. In the US, they were to be followed with equal interest, during the 1920s in particular. There the key figure was Walter Hagen, whom many would say was certainly the best matchplayer of his day and perhaps of all time.

Besides his successes in challenge matches, in the US PGA he has an unparalleled record in this period (it did not become a strokeplay event until 1958). Having been beaten on the 38th hole by Gene Sarazen in 1923, he then won it four years in a row – to add to an earlier victory in 1921. No one, between 1916 and 1957, came near Hagen's five victories – nearest were Gene Sarazen and Sam Snead, each with three successes.

Even so, the match victory that Hagen may have been the most proud of was over Bobby Jones in 1926. It was billed as the golf match of the century and in full measure it contained the element of settling who was the better of the two players. Most thought then, and the judgement of history is with them today, that Jones was. Nevertheless Hagen won overwhelmingly by 12 and 11, and this at a point in his career when it was beginning to be said that he was on the way down.

Another match was the prelude to the 1928 British Open. Hagen, out of practice having just crossed the Atlantic by liner in relaxed style – plenty of gambling and liquor – arrived at the Moor Park course to take on one of England's best golfers, the massive Archie Compston, in a £500 match over 72 holes. He was not so much beaten as annihilated. The score was 18 and 17. They continued playing, however, so that the spectators should not feel cheated of their entry money. Hagen then lost both the bye and the bye-bye.

Thoughtfully he went off to Sandwich to prepare for the British Open where, amongst a strong field, there would once again be Archie Compston. Little was heard of him during the days that followed as for once Hagen abandoned the bright lights and his 'little black book', dieted, took Turkish baths, and practised steadily, in the hope of rescuing something of his tarnished reputation.

The holder, Bobby Jones, was not in the field, but it was nevertheless a strong one. Tommy Armour, holder of the US Open, was there and, of the best Americans, so were Gene Sarazen, Jim Barnes and Wild Bill Mehlhorn. Argentine's José Jurado, the best golfer that South America was to produce until the advent of Roberto de Vicenzo, figured prominently throughout the championship. The Great Triumvirate – Vardon, Taylor and Braid – had all entered, but more in the sense of returning to scenes of former glories than with hopes of winning, for each of them was around sixty years of age. The main home hopes were centred firstly on Abe Mitchell, later to be assessed as the best golfer not to win a British Open, and George Duncan, who had beaten Hagen 6 and 5 in the first, but unofficial, match between Great Britain and the USA in 1926. He had won the Open on a nearby course in 1920, when Hagen had made his first appearance in Britain and finished last but one of the qualifiers. Finally there was a great name for the future of British golf, Henry Cotton, beginning to make a reputation for himself but with his first Open win six years into the future.

The entry was 271 players, some of whom, wrote Bernard Darwin, 'must have been moved to enter by a most singular delusion'. After the two qualifying rounds had been played they no doubt departed in sorrow. All the big names remained, not as when Gene Sarazen was blown out of the championship by high winds at Troon in 1923 (he was to return to that unhappy scene fifty years on in 1973, and had the same score, 160 for the first two rounds of the Open).

Wild Bill Mehlhorn took the lead after the first round with a 71, then – quite rightly – thought of as scoring almost as good as a mortal could do. Sarazen followed with 72, Jurado with 74 and amongst a group on 75 were Percy Alliss, George Duncan, Walter Hagen and Archie Compston. Hagen's round would have been better but the supreme putter of his generation had missed a couple of short ones. On the other hand, he had demonstrated something of his ability at scrambling it towards the hole. On the 13th he had pushed his second shot and then fluffed his third into a bunker. Nevertheless he was down for a 5. On the last he had found himself in thick greenside grass and with his first attempt to get it near the hole had hardly moved the ball. But he got his 5 again. Meanwhile, Harry Vardon had given one of the last glimpses of his quality by going out in 35, but he then returned in 43 – the agonised putting of all but his early years had probably once more been to blame.

The second day José Jurado managed only a 38 on the easier half of the course but then lashed his way home in 33. His halfway total of 145 put him three ahead of Hagen, who had 148, as did Sarazen. Compston was still there, the home country's best hope now, with 149.

Sarazen had begun unsteadily, dropping three strokes to strict par on the first five, but had still been out in 36 and finished with a 76. Sarazen later considered that one hole had already cost him the championship. He had taken 7 on the Suez Canal hole after unwisely taking a wood from a doubtful lie in the rough.

Hagen took the lead on the morning of the final day. He went out in 33, looking far more solemn than his usual self, had then produced a succession of 5s but had played the concluding holes strongly for a 72. Sarazen was one stroke more and was 221 to Hagen's 220, as also was Jurado who had drifted a little to 76. He had needed a 4 for 74 on the last hole but had put his second into a bunker and then three-putted. Compston too was still there – just. Over the first nine he had included a 7 on his card and a 5 at a par 3 but had managed a 73 and a three-round total of 222.

In the afternoon Jurado faded right away to an 80. Hagen, too, began badly, dropping shots over the first seven holes this time, but he was steadied by a 2 on the 8th and had the answer when he got into trouble for the rest of the round. On the 13th he chipped stone dead. On the 15th his second finished under the face of a bunker and just to get the ball out looked problem enough. Walter got it to within about 12ft of the hole. No one doubted he would hole the putt, and he did (this was the man who once, on being asked if holing a putt for a lot of money didn't make the whole thing almost impossible said, 'What? Miss a putt for $2,000? Not likely!').

That putt holed, there were no more alarms, and Walter cruised home to a 72, during which he had visited seven bunkers, and a final total of 292.

Only Sarazen or Compston could now hope to catch him. Compston took 37 to the turn, which gave him little chance over the more difficult inward half, and had to be content with a 73 and a total which was three strokes higher than Hagen's. Sarazen went doggedly round in par but the birdies did not come. He was probably not encouraged by the sight of Walter lounging in a polo coat, chatting relaxedly with the Prince of Wales as if the championship were already his. On the 69th hole he dropped a shot and that was that:

292   Hagen (75, 73, 72, 72)
294   Sarazen (72, 76, 73, 73)
295   Compston (75, 74, 73, 73)

Hagen took the trophy and made off eagerly towards the bright lights of Paris. After a week of championship golf, days of practice and that match with Compston he could now forget, he needed other diversions. Walter had taken the third, and the one he valued the most, of his four British Opens. He had decided on a strategy of playing safe and had indeed got through the four rounds without a 6 on his cards. He could now safely unlock the little black book of useful telephone numbers from his trunk.

Compston? He was never to win an Open but his match victory over Hagen was a kind of compensation. He was probably thankful that the return is less remembered. In the USA this time, and once more over 72 holes, Walter won by 8 and 7.

If But Once You
Don't Succeed . . .

E

'I feel like many peoples are with me' - the 1967 British Open

ONE day in 1953 Roberto de Vicenzo broke down and wept in his hotel room. As it happened, he had not just lost an Open Championship by three-putting the last green, hooking a drive out of bounds or fluffing the simplest of chips – afflictions that have come to grieve many of the great ones at crucial moments. No, Roberto had wept because he *knew* he was about to lose the British Open, although he was tied for the lead with Ben Hogan on 214. His putting was going to let him down again in the final afternoon round. All week his long, drawing wood shots had soared down the fairways (for many years Roberto was the best long driver in the world and very nearly the longest of them all), the irons, too, had been struck equally superbly. But once he was on the greens he had, at worst, thrown shots away, at best, failed to take his chances.

Roberto, alas, was right. Hogan won it; de Vicenzo's name was fifth, five strokes behind the winner and one behind Frank Stranahan, who had single-putted each of the last six greens.

De Vicenzo had first competed in 1948. In the years between then and his nineteenth visit in 1967 he had been second on one occasion, third five times, fourth once and sixth once; there had really been only one occasion when he had been out of it as the championship entered its later stages.

Now it was too late, perhaps years too late, for Vicenzo was forty-five and only Harry Vardon back in 1914, and Old Tom Morris earlier still, had won an Open at that age. He had a good, but not great record to look back on. He had won 130 tournaments and 30 national championships, but the championships had been minor ones that are ignored in the record books –

mostly of South American countries – and the same applied to many of his tournament successes. He had never won a major championship and could hardly have expected to any more. He was, he said, just over to 'see old friends'.

Nevertheless, he was not taking his preparations for the 1967 Open lightly. De Vicenzo had a devotion approaching that of Ben Hogan to the art and the delights of striking a golf ball as well as is humanly possible. Hogan liked to get away to remote parts of the practice ground and seek perfection; de Vicenzo was more companionable but it was still his routine to hit balls for four hours and then go out for a round once he was satisfied. He paid equal attention to his putting, but here there was something of a desperation about the hours spent. He was looking for a stroke that would get the ball into the hole more frequently, that would not break down when the pressures of competition were at a height. He did not hope for perfection.

De Vicenzo had just beaten Nicklaus in a TV match but that does not count for very much. He was not mentioned by the press as a likely winner before the event began and odds of 33–1 were offered against his winning.

The first-round leader was probably on offer at a considerably higher price. Lionel Platts came in with a 68, only one off taking the Hoylake course record; Nicklaus, fresh from winning the US Open and holder of the British title, had 71; de Vicenzo had a 70.

After two rounds the position was:

140 Devlin and Nicklaus
141 De Vicenzo, Hume, Platts and Boobyer
142 Jacklin (then a rising star)
143 Clark and Player

Amongst those with a chance as pressure increased were Doug Sanders, Harold Henning and Kel Nagle on 144.

In the third round the players not of the very highest class faded away; Nicklaus was steady, with a 71; Clive Clark, a young former Walker Cup man, came into strong contention for a major championship for the first time with a fine round of 69, which included four birdies on Hoylake's punishing last five holes. The rounds of the day, however, were by Gary Player and Roberto de Vicenzo, who in the calm air both had 67s.

Relatively few had been watching de Vicenzo as he set out that day. So often he had been in a position to challenge for the Open only to fail in the final stages. But the 67 was something different. Could, people asked, this at long last be Roberto's year? But could his putting hold up under the extreme pressure? Would his soaring, drawn long shots, as has happened on occasion to Palmer, begin to hook sharply into the rough at decisive moments? The fairways were perilously narrow.

His lead, too, was a narrow one: two shots on Gary Player, three on Nicklaus, four on Clark and Devlin. A wild hook, a drive that failed to draw back from right rough or out of bounds, putting less than competent, and de Vicenzo's lead would vanish.

He may have felt this really was his last chance, and certainly did not suffer the fears that had preceded his last-round encounter with Hogan fourteen years earlier. And there was something else too. Roberto said, 'I feel like many peoples are with me.' They were. For his pursuers their feelings were different: for Nicklaus there was awe; for Player a somewhat begrudged respect; it would be very nice to see young Clive Clark pull it off, but most felt he was too young and without experience at this level of competition. For Roberto there was love. It was doubtful if a partisan British crowd would have been entirely delighted to see even a British golfer beat him.

De Vicenzo tried to throw off his fears of the other contenders. He had looked at Player, he said later, and thought, 'What the hell? You can't be afraid of this little fellow.' Clark, playing with Nicklaus ahead of de Vicenzo and Player, seemed to have put himself out of it when he went out of bounds at the 1st (though he later came back strongly). Nicklaus, however, was into one of those patented final rounds of his, when he abandons the early caution he feels necessary to keep himself in with a chance until he can prove his confident superiority over the last stretch. He opened quietly but had a 2 on the 193yd 7th and then sent his second shot with a 4-iron to the back of the 492yd 8th green. He was now just two strokes behind de Vicenzo. The 14th and 16th might hold the key to the championship. At 515 and 529yd they were out of range to all but Nicklaus – and perhaps de Vicenzo. When he heard that Nicklaus had managed only a 5 on the 14th he said, 'He make his par like a good boy. I feel better now.'

Player had stayed with de Vicenzo over the first nine. The latter, indeed, had missed a couple of greens with his approaches early on but had chipped superbly and kept to par. On the 10th, de Vicenzo had gone further ahead – his putting, for once, had done it for him. He had holed for a birdie 3, while Player had three-putted from about 12ft. By the 12th Player was out of it, and eventually was to finish with a 74 for a total of 284 and joint third place.

Ahead, Nicklaus birdied the 529yd 16th and the 400yd final hole. He had gone round in 69 and had a total of 280. De Vicenzo knew that this should not be good enough. He had only to play the last three holes in level par to win.

On the 16th de Vicenzo also got home in two, although the hole was playing into the wind. His long tee shot had finished only a handful of yards from being out of bounds on the right, but then he had struck a 3-wood to the middle of the green. Steady play on the last two holes of Hoylake's punishing finish, the 418yd 17th and 400yd 18th, would win it for him now. At both holes he drove long and true. Each time he had only a 9-iron left for his shot to the green; each time it curved in and held safely and he was down in two putts. A 70 for a total of 278. Roberto de Vicenzo had at last taken the British Open. There has never been a more popular victory.

It has remained his one victory in a major championship, though the following year he played the round of his life in the US Masters. In the final round he went out in 31, put a pitching wedge within a yard of the 17th hole and sank the putt, but at the last pulled his 4-iron approach and went one over par for the hole. Nevertheless it was a 65 and there would be a play-off the next day. As de Vicenzo checked through his scorecard he saw only that 5 on the 18th. He failed to notice that his playing partner, Tommy Aaron, had put down a 4 instead of a birdie 3 on the 17th. There was no play-off; the 4 had to stand.

Nevertheless it was perhaps another kind of victory for Roberto de Vicenzo. Everyone remembers his misfortune whilst the winner has been almost forgotten. Poor old Roberto for losing; poor Bob Goalby – the winner in name only.

The caddie who won the Open - the 1932 British Open

Everyone knows how Gene Sarazen holed in 1 at the Postage Stamp hole at Troon in the 1973 British Open. And how the next day he put his tee shot into a greenside bunker and then holed the next. His competitive past in British Opens is less well known in our day.

Sarazen has for long made an almost yearly pilgrimage to the British Open, nowadays more to see old friends than with any idea of doing more than play two rounds before failing to qualify for the final stages. Earlier this century he had to come over his fair share of times before achieving success.

The first of his two wins in the US Open came in 1922 when he was an unknown. It made him one of the top American golfers with Walter Hagen and Bobby Jones. By 1930 Hagen and Jones had, between them, won the British title at seven out of the nine Opens played between 1922 and 1930. Their haul would undoubtedly have been even higher had they both competed every year – Jones usually played only when he was over for a Walker Cup match. Sarazen was the one who could not win it.

His first attempt had been disastrous indeed. After a 75, in the second qualifying round, he was confronted by very high winds. He performed quite creditably in the circumstances – 85 – and had then to sit and watch others overtake him as the wind died away. He did not qualify but, like General MacArthur, promised to return.

In 1928 at Royal St Georges, Sandwich, he had a good chance

of winning but took a 7 at the Suez Canal hole when, against his caddie's advice, he took wood from a poor lie, topped it a short distance only, and then repeated the error in fury.

In 1932 the championship returned to Sandwich, to the adjoining Prince's course. Once again he had the same caddie, Skip Daniels. Their relationship is a story in itself.

Daniels had aged in the years that had passed and when Sarazen met him again in practice week he decided that the old man looked too weak to carry a bag through six rounds and the hours of practice that would precede them. Feeling guilty, but saying to himself that business was business, he rejected the caddie that Walter Hagen had 'loaned' him in 1928 and chose a young man.

There was a constant clash of personalities. The younger caddie would thrust a club at Sarazen. Sometimes Sarazen would find himself short of the green but the caddie always remarked that it was the quality of Sarazen's shot that was to blame, not his selection of club.

Sarazen's game, though he had been in excellent form and was the bookies' favourite, went into decline. The odds against his winning went out to 25–1. It was suggested to him that, as Daniels was heartbroken and Sarazen was dissatisfied with his caddie, little would be lost by giving the old man another try. The partnership worked as it had done four years before. Sarazen was again striking the ball well and blossomed under the advice and encouragement Daniels gave him. The odds against his winning fell once more.

Sarazen ensured qualifying when he shot 73 in the first round, and was then heartened when he looked out of his hotel bedroom window on the morning of the second round to see Skip pushing his way through a gale on his way from green to green to chart the pin positions. Nothing was being left to chance.

For the first round proper the wind had dropped and the conditions were relatively easy. Although the course, at nearly 7,000yd, was a long one for the 1930s, the fairways were running and the greens easy in pace. Sarazen went straight to the front with a 4-under-par round of 70 and was never over the right

figure at any hole. In the second round he equalled the course
record with a 69. He had four birdies in the last seven holes and
would have had five if he had holed from 6ft on the last green.
Accustomed as we have since become to scores in the mid 60s on
courses that have long been stretched, such scoring may seem
little more than competent. It is as well to remember that most
sportsmen and athletes play only as well as they have to in order
to beat their contemporaries. Four rounds averaging even par
was almost invariably good enough to win comfortably, and to
our eyes the par of a course was generous, particularly with
regard to the par 5s. Prince's, for instance, had five of them on
the card that year but their lengths were only 460, 453, 456, 516
and 460yd. Sarazen had six birdies on these holes during his first
two rounds.

We can perhaps put the level of Sarazen's achievement by the
halfway stage, with 139, into better perspective if we think of
the winning scores at Sandwich since the Open had become a
72-hole event. They were: 326, 310, 296, 303, 300 and 292.
Sarazen looked to be heading for a total not much worse than
280.

He had not, however, completely outpaced the field. His 139
was followed by Percy Alliss on 142; Archie Compston, C. A.
Whitcombe and W. H. Davies on 144; the defending champion,
Tommy Armour, was on 145 together with Arthur Havers and
Fred Robson; and Henry Cotton, with 146, was not out of it.
Macdonald Smith had opened with a 71, but on the 1st in his
second round had hooked into a bunker, thrashed his attempted
recovery hard into the face, and then been forced to play out
backwards and eventually reached the green of this 382yd hole
in five shots – a 7. His total for the round was 76, and eight
strokes was too much leeway to make up, even when every
winner of an Open was expected to have one poor round.

Sarazen was out at nine o'clock on the final day. His first half
of 33 put the championship more firmly in his grasp and he
came home in a 1-under-par 37 for a round of 70 and a three-
round total of 209.

Playing about two hours behind Sarazen, Arthur Havers,

winner of the Open in 1923, made his thrust with the lowest round of the championship – a 68. Like most rounds of golf, it could have been better. He had gone out as well as Sarazen with a 33, but had three-putted the 14th and missed a fairly short putt on the last. A 66 would really have given Sarazen something to think about but Havers remained Sarazen's closest – and indeed the only likely – challenger, four shots behind. Macdonald Smith, with a 71, had pulled back to third place, but was eight shots to the bad.

If Sarazen could continue to play the same brand of golf, the championship was his for the taking. His play had indeed caught the attention of everyone. He was, as always and despite his lack of height, long off the tee, so much so that he often drove with a spoon (3-wood) to hold the hard, undulating fairways better, and even then seldom needed more than a long iron for his second shot. Again and again he had sent these rifling in to nestle a handful of yards from the flag. Then he had struck the ball almost dangerously boldy at the hole, confident that he could hole any return putt.

Sarazen began his final round steadily enough with three pars and a birdie before dropping a shot on the 217yd 5th. Another shot went at the 391yd 7th. He was now faced with the hole he felt presented the greatest threat. It was a possible birdie-4 hole, at 453yd, but easy to take 6 or worse. After the drive a golfer usually had to play from a downhill lie and had to take a wood to reach the green. Barring his way, and lying a little less than 100yd from the green, was a chain of bunkers rising to more than 30ft in height. It was all too easy to fail to get the ball up from the testing lie; if you scuttled it along the ground and finished in the bunkers, it was very unlikely that you could get your third shot on to the green. They were also a graveyard for those that hit a true shot which then failed to rise quickly enough. If the ball plugged into the face, a 7 immediately became the likely outcome.

Skip Daniels paused to consider the possibilities before deciding that Sarazen could be trusted with the spoon. The resulting shot they both thought was the best Sarazen had played during the championship. When they got to the green there was the ball about 9ft from the pin. Down went the putt for an eagle. Sarazen now had the 1932 British Open in the palms of his hands but his fingers had yet to close on it.

He completed the outward half in 35 and turned for home. A shot was dropped on the 10th but then three pars followed and then a 2 on the 202yd 14th. Sarazen could now afford to relax and seemed to do so. He three-putted the 15th and then hit a poor chip on the next but finished 5, 4 against a par of 5, 5. He was round in 74 for a total of 283, two strokes better than Bobby Jones's record 285 in the 1927 British Open at St Andrews.

Havers needed a 70 to tie but no one gave him much chance, despite the 68 of the morning. Perhaps if he had a good start . . . Havers began 5, 4, 3, 5 against strict par of 4, 4, 3, 4 and had a par 5 at the 8th as against Sarazen's eagle two hours before. His 37 to the turn was obviously not good enough, for the second half had a par of 38. So it proved. He finished in 76 and was pushed into third place by Macdonald Smith, who had a closing 70 which still left him five strokes behind Sarazen.

Besides setting a scoring record and leading all the way – both extremely rare achievements – Sarazen had managed to do something even rarer. Throughout the four rounds he had not played any one hole particularly badly. To prove it, there was not a single 6 on his cards.

He asked officials if Daniels might stand by his side for the presentation ceremony but was told that this was not possible. After all, it was just recently that professional golfers themselves had been allowed to put a foot inside a British clubhouse.

Perhaps Sarazen had been right a couple of weeks before when he thought Daniels too old for the strains of an Open. A few months later the old man was dead.

Not by length alone – the 1966 British Open

Gary Player thought Muirfield's 6,887yd made up the finest Open Championship test he had seen in a very long time indeed. What the organisers had done was to put a premium on control of length and straightness by what, to me, are rather rough-and-ready means. 'Rough' was in fact the key word in their strategy.

It had been allowed to grow around the greens so that an approach that was quite good but not exact was likely to finish in grass 2–3in deep. The lies players were likely to get were not bad, but the chip shots from crisp turf that tournament professionals have become so expert at were now far more difficult. When bedded in grass, the ball cannot normally be struck with nearly as much backspin – it tends to skid out and usually rolls and rolls once it reaches the putting surface. And then again, if a golfer decides to abandon his pitching or sand wedge for these close-up shots and putt or use a straight-faced iron, whenever there are no bunkers or humps between him and the hole, he is likely to find that there will be too much grass between the blade of his club and the ball as he comes into his shot. How far his ball will travel again becomes a matter of fine judgement – and luck.

Straightness from the tee was perhaps even more vital than accuracy with the approach shot. The grass had been allowed to grow so that a wayward shot into the rough did not finish in a lie that might be every bit as good as a fairway one. Jack Nicklaus, surveying the scene from a tee, thought that the rough looked like wheat whipping in the wind – it was 1½ft deep in places.

A special penalty had been imposed on long hitters if they did not keep as straight as they were long. At past the 250yd mark, the fairways had been narrowed to no more than 25yd, whereas before this point they were considerably wider. The long hitters were either going to have to risk their only mildly off-line shots finding heavy lies from which they would often not be able to force the ball to the green, or take 3-woods and irons from the tee in order to keep short of the narrowed stretches of fairway.

All this was merely following recent practice for the US Open. Many tournaments on the US circuit are played on courses which offer wide expanses for the tee shot. The tournament then becomes a contest which is primarily about walloping the ball a very long way in the general direction of the green and the winner thereafter is the man who is using his wedge and putter the best that particular week. The same kind of alterations as those made at Muirfield had been put into effect earlier for the US Open. There was, however, one significant difference which made Muirfield's narrowed fairways more demanding than would usually be the case with an American course: their hard, links-type undulations more often threw a good shot at a tangent into the rough. The more lush inland courses over which the US Open is usually played have fairways that hold shots which pitch on them.

By 1966 the British Open had become a kind of world championship of golf, mainly, I think, because it attracted a more international field than the US Open. (In the latter championship in 1975, for instance, only four non-Americans competed: Gary Player of South Africa, Peter Oosterhuis and Tony Jacklin of England and Robert Panasiuk of Canada; by contrast, about forty countries were represented in the British Open of that year.) In 1966 the field was formidable indeed – perhaps as strong as any up to that time.

The favourite, as usual, was Jack Nicklaus, who had still to win the British. Then there was twice-winner Arnold Palmer; Gary Player, who had taken it as his first major championship in 1959; the previous year's and five-times winner, Peter Thomson, eager to make it six and equal Harry Vardon's record; Bruce Devlin of Australia, who was overdue to win a major championship; Kel Nagle, winner of the Centenary Open in 1960; Tony Lema, who had virtually stepped off a trans-Atlantic flight on to the course and won in 1964; Roberto de Vicenzo, who had come close so often; and well-fancied Americans such as Phil Rodgers, Doug Sanders, Julius Boros and Dave Marr. No one had very high hopes of a British player carrying off the championship but the golfer with the best chance was probably David Thomas, still perhaps the longest *straight* driver of his time, who had come as close as a play-off in 1958, one of Thomson's years.

No one came near defeating the course the first day, and at the end of it two players led with 70 – Jack Nicklaus and Jimmy Hitchcock, an Englishman. Sanders, Harold Henning and Lema followed one stroke behind and then came Player, Nagle and Thomas with 72s. Amongst those with 73 were Boros, Thomson, Marr, Palmer, Peter Butler and Devlin. No unknown had jumped into a first-round lead; none of the great ones had put himself out of contention.

The contest between power and straightness had balanced out quite evenly. Nicklaus, for instance, seldom used his driver from the tees but his power enabled him still to get home at the longer holes with a couple of iron shots. He and the other long hitters such as de Vicenzo, Palmer and Thomas might indeed be getting themselves into the deep rough more often but, once there, they were more able to slash a clubhead through the grass and the ball.

On the second day Nicklaus made it his best opening pair of rounds in five attempts. After a 67 he led by a shot from Peter Butler who, though underpowered, had done everything else right. He had led at the halfway stage in a US Masters; now he had a 65, the lowest round of the tournament. Could he keep it up? The answer, sadly, was no. The next day he was to take fifteen strokes more and on the last day had a 75 to finish on 293 – not bad, but very much out of it. At the start of the third round Nicklaus was three strokes better than those who came behind Butler – Rodgers, who had produced almost the round of the day, a 66, Henning and Nagle; Sanders followed them with 141.

None of the well-fancied players had yet disappeared from view, however. Boros, for example, making his first appearance in a British Open, was on 144; Devlin, 142, and Palmer, 145 (could he come back after the trauma of having just lost the US Open to Billy Casper when the thing had looked all over?).

Halfway through the third round, it looked as if Nicklaus was going to cruise home comfortably. Playing solid, assured golf, he was still level par after the 13th. On the next he failed to get down in two from a bunker and thereafter the shots leaked away. He did not play badly; it was more that his irons into the greens finished just short or just through and he could not get the ball into the hole in two more shots. The collars of rough around the greens were taking the toll intended.

Meanwhile two players in particular took the second half of Muirfield apart – Palmer and Rodgers. Palmer, after 37 out, came home in 32. Rodgers, seeming, like Butler, to be feeling ill-effects from his brilliant round of the day before, had gone to the turn in 40. That must be him out of it. But no, he then pro-ceeded to set a new record for nine holes of a British Open. He came back in 30. That meant a total for the three rounds of 210. Nicklaus, who had finished with 75, was no longer three better than Rodgers, but two strokes behind. Palmer's round had pulled him up through the field and he lay at 214, as did David Thomas who had also gone round in 69. One stroke ahead of this pair and lying third was Doug Sanders. These seemed cer-tain to be the main protagonists on the final day (this was the first year that the final 36 holes of the Open were not played on one day). There were others – Henning, Player, Devlin, Nagle, Marr, Sebastian Miguel and Thomson – not wholly out of touch but their hopes rested on the leaders stumbling.

Nicklaus and Rodgers were out last, with Palmer and Sanders immediately in front; ahead of them, Thomas and Henning. Nicklaus at once had the kind of start that must have dismissed from many minds some of the doubts caused by his weak finish of the previous day. He ran a putt of about 8yd into the hole for a birdie and, even more important, in the space of a single hole he was level with Phil Rodgers, who had taken 5 at this 429yd hole. For the leaders there were no spectacular triumphs or disasters during the rest of the first half, although Henning faded out of it. Thomas was playing steadily and so too was Nicklaus. He had a putt of 3ft on the 495yd 9th for a birdie and to be out in 32, but he missed. After he had parred the 10th he was three strokes better than Thomas and four up on Rodgers and Sanders (despite an eagle from 60yd by the latter at the 9th). By this time Palmer was virtually out of it. He had got into the rough at this 475yd hole, had been over-optimistic in his choice of club from the lie, and the result for him at the 10th was a 7.

Nicklaus was back in command of the championship. Then,

on the par-4 11th, he lined up a putt of 7ft for a birdie. His ball finished 15in away. Again he lined it up with his usual massive deliberation. Again he missed. Ahead, Thomas had holed for a 2 on the 154yd 13th. Nicklaus, who at his best aims to fade his shots from left to right, then hooked hugely from the 12th tee. But he was in luck. His ball cleared the rough paralleling the fairway and came to rest on ground where the grass had been trodden flat by spectators. He got his second shot on to the green and two-putted for a par. At the par-3 13th he wavered again. He was short of the green from the tee and then too strong with his chip and took 4.

Thomas, for the first time in the championship, now had a real chance. If he could set a stiff target, Nicklaus might have trouble earning the right to a play-off. He did just this by finishing in another 69 for a four-round total of 283. He played the last four holes in par but had missed a 7ft putt for a birdie on the 198yd 16th and had failed to get to the 528yd 17th in two, as his length of shot had made quite possible.

From the 14th tee Nicklaus pushed his drive into a bunker, so that the green of this 462yd hole was out of reach. Another shot dropped. At this point he heard that Thomas was in at 283 and that Sanders, playing the 18th, would probably return the same total. Nicklaus now needed level par to the end to tie these scores. On the 15th his approach was a little weak and he found himself some 14yd short of the flag. He had difficulty in getting down in two more but nevertheless a 4 went down on his card.

Club selection was a problem on the 198yd 16th. In a wind, the yardage of a shot is no more important than wind direction. At this hole it was coming from directly behind the player. Too big a club and he would be through the green and, even with a fairly lofted club, the ball would run quite a long way as the following wind would decrease the backspin on the ball. Nicklaus erred on the side of caution and took out a 7-iron. He was on the green but had a 10yd putt to the hole. He stroked it decisively and his ball finished only an inch or so away. To have a tap-in putt of that kind of length is a welcome relief for a player at a crucial stage of a championship.

Page 85 Muscle power: *(above)* Peter Thomson, 1967; *(below left)* Ben Hogan, 1953; *(below right)* Arnold Palmer, 1971

Nicklaus relates in his book *The greatest game of all* that his spirits lifted at this point and that he began to think more positively. Now it was not for him a question of whether or not he could finish in par to earn a tie and play-off with Sanders and Thomas the next day. He began to think in terms of winning outright.

On the 528yd 17th the tee shot was played to an upward-sloping fairway so that the ball disappeared from sight as it reached the landing zone. The hole then swung to the left and about 100yd from the green a ridge of high bunkers encroached from the right. Thereafter, there was a channel leading through rough on one side and broken ground on the other.

Nicklaus took a 3-iron from the tee. If he drove too far, he might reach the rough at the angle of the fairway. With the 3-iron he stopped only a couple of yards short of it. Again there was a difficult decision as to choice of club with the wind behind. He was about 240yd out and he relates that he took various factors into account, deducting a full club for this, and a half club for that – wind strength, small British ball and the fact that a player excited by prospects of victory hits any shot perhaps 20yd further than his norm. After these thoughts Nicklaus came down from taking a 1- or 2-iron to a 5. He brought his ball to rest about 5yd from the flag and two putts gave him the birdie that had escaped Thomas. Now a par on the 429yd 18th would give him his first British Open.

Again Nicklaus took an iron from the tee and left himself with an approach of just over 200yd. This time the wind was not behind and he took a 3-iron and finished in the heart of the green. He putted up to less than 1ft and the Open was his:

```
282   Nicklaus (70, 67, 75, 70)
283   Thomas (72, 73, 69, 69)
283   Sanders (71, 70, 72, 70)
286   Player, Devlin, Nagle and Rodgers
```

Trevino feels that he has little chance in the Masters. He feels that the course favours hookers, while he works the ball from left to right. Nicklaus, as regards the British Open, had not been pessimistic about his chances to the same degree, but he did feel that it was the most difficult of the four major championships for him to win for not dissimilar reasons. Nicklaus hits high, even towering, shots which are far more affected by wind than the low shots of a Trevino or Palmer.

What the organisers felt about the result is, as far as I know, not recorded. They had aimed to put a premium on control and penalise length that was not ruthlessly straight. Yet two of the longest hitters in the field, Nicklaus and Thomas, had finished first and second and had played the course very differently from the tee at that. Thomas had stayed with his driver for a high proportion of the time off the tees. Nicklaus had not. On only one hole, the 516yd 5th, had he always used a driver regardless of wind direction; otherwise he used it only on a few of the par 4s in what he felt were suitable winds. In the four rounds, he says that he took a driver only seventeen times as against ten 3-woods. His remaining twenty-nine tee shots at the par 4s and 5s were mostly made with 1-irons and the occasional 3-iron. The trick was that he knew that he could still get home to the green with the accuracy of an iron for his second shot. Others had to drive from a tee to avoid having to take woods for their seconds.

The idea had not been to stop Nicklaus winning, however, but to ensure that neither he nor anyone else won merely because of a knack of hitting the ball a very long way. Nicklaus had proved that, awesome as his power might be, there was a whole lot more to his game than that.

Eyeball to Eyeball

Fairy tales can come true - the 1955 US Open

THERE are a very few golf encounters that have, on the instant, become folklore and legend. One of these undoubtedly was the 1913 US Open play-off between the Goliaths Harry Vardon and Ted Ray, and David in the person of Francis Ouimet. The fact that it was the stuff of folklore is, if we think about it, proved. No one at all, either before the encounter or after it, ever wrote a single word about the drama of a match between Ray and Vardon. At Brookline, Massachusetts, the greatest British golfer was out to beat Ted Ray, who had won the British Championship the previous year. But no, that side of it was, and is, ignored and we have always had the contest portrayed as Young America *v* the Masters from the Old World. This despite the fact that Vardon and Ray probably did not, for a while, see it in that light at all and busied themselves watching each other. More fool them. They should have been more wary of what a good scriptwriter like God could make out of it.

To me, the other encounter that contains similar ingredients, in much the same measures, is the 1955 US Open. In writing about golf one is always involved in a wealth of not very illuminating statistics which, nevertheless, just have to be there. Sometimes, however, these do seem to have less than their usual importance: the match of Bobby Jones *v* Cyril Tolley in the 1930 British Amateur, when *how* Jones or Tolley won a particular hole was far more important than the actual scores for it, is an example. Fleck *v* Hogan in 1955 has the same character, though there is otherwise little similarity in the encounters.

Jack Fleck came to the Olympic Club with no sort of reputation. He was a professional at two municipal courses in Iowa. Occasionally he played in tournaments and once he had finished as high as sixth. At Olympic he had played poorly during practice, even going round in 87 in one round. He started as a complete outsider.

In the field was Ben Hogan, with Bobby Jones, Jack Nicklaus and Arnold Palmer, the greatest of American golfers. In 1953 he had achieved a kind of Grand Slam in winning the Masters and the US and British Opens. The PGA was beyond him – the dates clashed with the British Open and he had chosen to go to Carnoustie. Now, in 1955, he was bidding to become the first man to win the US Open five times. If he had done it, he would have been one up on Bobby Jones and Willie Anderson. The latter really did not count anyway as his victories had come between 1901 and 1905, when any golfer with the ability of a present-day 4-handicapper would have won with strokes to spare.

Olympic was a course much menaced by wiry rough and hosts of pine, eucalyptus and cypress. More balls were to be lost there than in any other US Open and drives carried only an average 216yd. To add to these difficulties, for the first time collars of rough were allowed to grow around the green to penalise shots that were quite good but not good enough. No wonder that observers felt Hogan was playing less freely, his swing tight, shorter, more controlled. They were probably right. He was aiming to place the ball *there* and then *there* rather than go for the long tee shot; it was essential to always keep the ball in play.

Statistics cannot be totally ignored, so it had better be said that Hogan played the first three rounds in 72, 73, 72 and failed to have the Open won at that point because he bogeyed each of the last three holes in his third round. This gave him a one-shot lead over Sam Snead and Julius Boros, with Fleck three behind him. He had scored a 76 to open with, had a third round of 75, but had managed to get a 69 from somewhere in between. It had been one of very, very few rounds below 70 in the championship and there was really no chance that he would do it again. Tommy Bolt, for instance, had a 67 in the first round and had followed it with a 77, still good enough to give him the joint lead with Harvie Ward after two rounds. But Hogan, the inevitable and inexorable, was there all the time, plugging away a stroke or two over 70.

In the final round Ben Hogan played his best golf of the championship – 70. When he got back to the clubhouse to await the rest of the field he was five strokes better than anyone else who had finished. There was an hour to wait until the whole thing was over and Hogan could receive the cup as a five-times winner. There were many ready to congratulate him on his victory, but Hogan waved them all away. He was sure that he had won but he knew just as surely that fate must not be mocked.

Had not Gene Sarazen once upon a time suddenly produced a double eagle, late on, and gone on to tie for the Masters?

As it turned out, only Jack Fleck had any sort of a chance with a few holes to play. Quite a possible one in fact. So well had he played in the final round that he needed only to be one under par on the last six holes to tie Hogan's score. But people who have finished no higher than sixth in major competition play are not at all likely to sustain an effort in the run-up to the finish.

Jack Fleck parred the 13th, bogeyed the 14th, and on the 15th forced in a 9ft putt for a 2. He still needed two pars and a birdie on the last three holes.

The 16th measured over 600yd. Fleck, not surprisingly, did not reach the heart of the green in two but he was on the edge in three. He very nearly holed out from there, but got a solid par. The 17th was a long par 4 – over 460yd. Fleck was some 13 or 14yd past the hole with his second shot and his birdie putt spun round the rim. Another par, and now he needed that birdie on the last hole of all. Not impossible, since the hole was one of the easier par 4s, at only 337yd. His drive was a good one but drawn just a few inches into the wiry rough. This made it more diffi-cult to stop on the green, let alone near the pin. Bobby Jones's shot of 170yd from sand to win an Open has gone down in history. Jack Fleck had a shot to play that was not a touch easier. He had to come out of the rough, clear a rise in front of him, clear a greenside bunker, and then stop his ball on a narrow stretch of green, short of another bunker. He took out a 7-iron and did just that.

That he should hole the 8ft putt was now inevitable, in terms of fairy tales, and of course he did. A tie. Fleck stood swaying on his feet. Later, in the press tent, he was speechless – former Open Champion Ed Furgol had to speak for him.

Later there have been those to say that Hogan could not win a play-off; that his thinking was conditioned to lasting four rounds and no more; that after his 1949 crippling accident four rounds was his physical limit. But what did it look like to Jack Fleck? He had tied for the Open and now he had to play against the greatest golfer of his era. How could he hope for the magic spell to continue?

But the heroes of most fairy tales are not daunted by this sort of prospect, and Jack Fleck was no lesser man than they.

The first four holes passed without particular drama. On the 5th Hogan put a shot behind a tree. One up to Fleck. On the next there followed a hooked approach into a bunker and a 25ft putt holed. Then on the 8th Hogan, by this time in his career not even a good putter, holed from something like 16yd for a 2. On the next Fleck birdied from 8yd and then from 6yd at the next. This meant that he was three strokes ahead with eight holes to play.

What was Hogan going to do about it? As much as he could. He had a birdie at the 14th and another at the 17th and all was contrived very nicely indeed for the last hole – Fleck one stroke ahead with one hole to play. How would you write a script for what was to happen next? Not, I think, one that included any of the events that followed.

Hogan is said to have hooked from the tee because 'his foot slipped'. I cannot myself imagine that Hogan, on a tee, on a normal sort of a day, would look at the grass and then deliber-ately plant his feet on anything that, even just possibly, he might slip on. Whatever the truth of the matter, he definitely did hook into deep rough and just as definitely did Jack Fleck hit his shot down the fairway and put his second a few yards from the hole. Meanwhile, Hogan, obviously doomed to be the Ugly Sister of this fairy tale, marched to his ball which *happened* to be buried in just about the only small patch of rough that no one had *happened* to think worth cutting all week. His first wedge shot merely let him see where the ball was. His second moved it a foot or two. With his third wedge, he was on the fairway. Thereafter fate was a little kinder to him. He put his fifth shot on the green but, as he was no doubt weary of hitting balls not very far on that particular hole, about 10yd past the hole. The next putt, a curling down-hiller, was quite impossible. Hogan holed it for a 6. Jack Fleck got down without further unnecessary drama in two putts. He had won with 69 to Hogan's 72.

The end of the fairy story – except that Hogan had still to win his fifth Open and obviously he, more than anyone, deserved to have this achievement next to his name. The next year, without Jack Fleck to worry him, he missed a short putt on the last green to tie with Cary Middlecoff, who had produced a fairy-tale finish of his own of 68, 68.

We then go forward to 1960, Hogan's last chance and the year that Arnold Palmer's finishing 65 gave him his first US Open. But I doubt that Ben Hogan had Palmer in mind as he came towards the last few holes at Cherry Hills. On the 17th it looked to Hogan as if, five years later, there, once again, was Jack Fleck, getting in the way of destiny. Fleck had birdied five of the first six holes, obviously ready to write another fairy tale into golf history. On the 548yd 17th it seemed to Hogan that he had to get a birdie to beat Fleck. To do it required a third shot that would just clear the water in front of the green and stop near the hole. It cleared the water and spun back – into the water. Hogan managed a 6 from there but that was obviously that. Once again Fleck had beaten him. This time Fleck's 283 was worth not even a footnote in history, for his total gave him third place only, with Hogan on 284.

Local boy makes good – the 1913 US Open

Miller, Trevino, Nicklaus, Weiskopf, Player: few would disagree that these are the biggest names in international golf in the mid 1970s. All except one are American. In 1913 the names were Vardon, Taylor, Braid and Ray. All were British, and all played most of their golf in the British Isles. When any one of them ventured overseas it was to show the natives how the game should be played. If they competed in a championship, the question was which of them would come first. The Frenchman in France or the American in the US might hope to finish well up the field but to win was the stuff that dreams are made of.

Harry Vardon made his second exhibition tour of the US in 1913, accompanied by Ted Ray, the 1912 British Open Champion. Wherever they went, crowds flocked. Was not Vardon incomparably the greatest player the game had yet seen? Even today, perhaps with Joyce Wethered, his swing is still thought of as the most graceful and easy the game has known. His accuracy gave birth to a host of stories. He could place a brassie shot as near the pin as a modern master with a wedge. It was said, and widely believed, that he could not play the same course twice in a day without experiencing a problem that never faced other players. The second time round his tee shots at the par 4s and 5s were said to come to rest in the divots left by his second shots of the morning round. Playing the par 3s was even worse: he had to putt out of the pitch marks left on the greens by his earlier iron shots.

Ted Ray was an attraction of a different kind. True, he did not quite rank with the Great Triumvirate, as they were called, of Vardon, Taylor and Braid, because his championship record in the British Open was considerably inferior to theirs, but of these figures of the dim golfing past he, more than anyone else, had something of the crowd appeal that Arnold Palmer was to have in the 1950s and 1960s. Not for either of them a steady progress down the centre of the fairway and a predictable arrival at the fat of the green. The ordinary golfer could identify with Ted Ray. His ball also frequently came to rest behind trees, in bunkers and not often visited parts of the rough. But the similarity ended there. Ted, like Arnold Palmer, was a player of great power. His swing was not pretty – some called it a combination of lurch and heave – but it did smash a clubhead into the ball.

And if not too large a sapling lay between him and it, he could deal with that too. So golfing galleries gasped as his ball soared over trees and out of bunkers or flew up out of the rough together with prodigious turves.

In September 1913, the Englishmen interrupted their tour to call in on the US Open Championship at Brookline Country Club. Gathered to meet them was a host of hopeful rather than confident Americans – whatever they may have said for the benefit of the press. Some of these were not native-born but, like Jim Barnes the Cornishman, and Macdonald Smith, a Scotsman, had emigrated to the money and better status enjoyed by the professional golfers of the US. There was, however, 'Hagin, a home-bred American of whom no one seems to have heard much', as Bernard Darwin of *The Times* put it. It was a name that would soon be well known on both sides of the Atlantic, and in a day or so Darwin had got his spelling right. Walter Hagen already thought he was as good as anyone, though he had yet to make up his mind to concentrate on either golf or baseball. His performance in this his first national tournament nearly decided him, but much of the field was of poor quality – Darwin commented, 'Many of the players supply irrefutable evidence that the word "professional" is not always synonymous with "good".'

The 36-hole qualifying was split into two days. No one was much surprised when Vardon led the first day's qualifiers on 151 and Ted Ray led the second group, but three strokes better. Already, some of the Americans must have been wondering which of the two Englishmen would be the eventual winner, though Hagen felt he had not disgraced himself with 157 and a young American amateur with the unlikely name of Francis Ouimet had made the best use of his local-boy knowledge to total 152. He had probably burned himself out and the 72 holes of the championship proper were yet to begin.

The scores followed a predictable pattern for the first two rounds, at which point Vardon and Wilfred Reid, another Englishman, led on 147, followed by Ray on 149, after a tournament-best round of 70; the Anglo-Americans Macdonald and

Barnes were on 150. And then came the first native Americans, Hagen and Ouimet. Ouimet was still there after the third round and was tied for the lead with both Vardon and Ray on 225.

In the final round Ray faltered to a 79 but he was the leader in the clubhouse (it is only quite recently that leaders have gone out together). The rest of the field would have to withstand the tension of having 'only' 304 to beat.

Never a good putter in his later years, Vardon played well through the green but also returned a 79. Barnes, Smith and Hagen faded out over the second 9. Hagen's last fling for the title had contained a wealth of variety. He had begun, 6, 5, 7 against a par of 4, 4, 4. During practice he had observed Vardon's swing. His own was not going well, so he would try Vardon's to see if that would work better for him. An eagle 2 followed at the next and then a birdie. Much better. He then birdied the 6th and parred the 7th. Hagen now seemed to be back in contention but thought he had again put himself out of it when he dropped shots at each of the next two holes to reach the turn in 40. However, he then heard that Vardon and Ray were doing no better. They turned in 42 each. The three were level with nine holes to go. On the 13th Hagen had a medium-length putt to go into the lead, but it slipped by. The 14th finished his chances. Ahead, Vardon and Ray had both birdied it, and Hagen could have reached the green with his second but decided to risk a brassie shot from the wet turf; it fizzed along the ground for just a few yards. Next he went for the green with a long iron and hooked it. In the end there was a 7 to go down on Hagen's card and the three strokes dropped to Vardon and Ray on this hole were the final margin between them.

Meanwhile, Ouimet seemed headed for not much better than 90. He took 43 to the turn and then dropped two more strokes on the par-3 10th. He parred the next and then dropped yet another stroke. He had to cover the last six holes in two under par and the course was playing long and was in a near-water-logged state. On the 13th he chipped in for a birdie. He had to struggle for his pars on the next three holes and with two holes to go had to find a birdie on one of them. He got it with a downhill, sidehill putt of some 5yd on the 17th. He had only to par the last hole to tie with Vardon and Ray. He did so fairly comfortably. It was a story too unlikely to have been given space in a *Boys' Own*. The twenty-year-old local boy had tied the English multi-champions. It was as if today a 2-handicap golfer matched, say, Miller and Nicklaus stroke for stroke. The one parallel I can think of came in the 1921 British Open when Roger Wethered forced a play-off with the eventual winner, Jock Hutchison, and then capped the story by expressing doubts about whether he could stay on an extra day for it. He had agreed to play for his village in a cricket match and felt he ought to honour his word.

But Wethered, though also an amateur, was one of the two best, with Cyril Tolley, of his day. Francis Ouimet was almost an unknown, though he did hold his state's amateur championship and had reached the semi-final of the US Amateur. He awoke on 20 September 1913 to newspaper fame, but at the course there were few takers at the 10–1 odds against his beating Vardon and Ray in the 18-hole play-off.

Francis went over to the practice ground and hit some warm-up shots out to his ten-year-old caddy Eddie Lowery, until he was told that Vardon and Ray were awaiting him at the 1st tee. The first crisis of the day concerned Eddie. Francis was stopped by a friend, a golfer of experience, who offered to caddy for him. Obviously his advice might be useful during the pressures of the day. He told the friend to get Eddie's agreement which the boy refused to give, even when he was offered a bribe. When Ouimet saw tears coming into his eyes he said, 'Eddie's going to caddy for me.'

In a steady drizzle that followed hours of heavy rain Ouimet, Vardon and Ray drew straws for the honour. Ouimet teed off first. 'Be sure and keep your eye on the ball,' Eddie Lowery advised. Francis put his drive safely down the middle and felt some of the tension drain away. In the heavy conditions none of them could reach the 430yd par 4 in two, and three 5s went down on the cards. Vardon and Ouimet parred the 2nd and 3rd, where Ray dropped a stroke. Ted was playing erratically. After pushing his drives off the first three tees, he hooked at the 4th hole.

The 5th brought Francis Ouimet his first crisis of the round from his first real error. He sliced his brassie second out of bounds. Without a change of expression he dropped another ball and put it on the green with the same club. He got down in two more and in fact each of the players took 5. (At the time, the penalty for going out of bounds was just the wasted shot rather than the later, more severe penalty of stroke and distance.) Francis had lost no ground, saved by the accuracy of his second attempt.

Vardon birdied the next, which put him a shot up on Francis and two on Ted Ray. By the 8th they were all level. Francis hit a mid iron dead at the flag and holed from about 18in. Vardon had a par 4 and Ray holed a long one for a birdie. They all had par 5s at the 9th, so at the halfway stage their cards read as follows:

Ouimet   38 (5, 4, 4, 4, 5, 4, 4, 3, 5)
Vardon   38 (5, 4, 4, 4, 5, 3, 4, 4, 5)
Ray   38 (5, 4, 5, 4, 5, 4, 3, 3, 5)
Par   36 (4, 4, 4, 4, 4, 4, 3, 4, 5)

Not great scoring certainly but the course was waterlogged in part so there was never any run on a tee shot. Every shot was all carry. The equipment they played with left much to be desired. Modern steel shafts can hardly be improved on but the player of today still seeks the greater distance that a lighter shaft can give. So aluminium, fibreglass and carbon fibre have been tried and, to some extent at least, have not given the final answer. But how would a Nicklaus or Miller handle hickory-shafted woods and irons with those thin blades that allowed no margin for error? Probably pretty well, once they learned to compensate for the lateral twisting of the shaft on any full shot, but the fact that they would never be able to hit full out would cost them an average of something like five shots a round. A 79 today rules a player out of nearly any tournament, but when Ray and

Vardon completed their fourth rounds in 79 each, as we have seen, this was still good enough to tie. Championships were to be won with four-round totals of more than 300 for many years yet.

At the 140yd 10th Ouimet took the lead for the first time. All three had hit the green but both Vardon and Ray three-putted. On the 12th Ouimet had the chance of gaining two shots on Vardon and Ray but he was short with his birdie putt while they were taking bogey 5s. Vardon then birdied the next to pull himself back to only one shot behind Ouimet.

The pressure now began to tell. Each player faltered on the 14th. Vardon hooked off the tee, recovered well, and then again hooked with his approach. Ray pushed his long second well out to the right. Ouimet failed to benefit, as he topped his second, but played a good iron to the green and the hole was halved in par 5s. Ray was lucky on the next hole. His tee shot was flying well into the rough when it struck a spectator and ricocheted back on to the fairway. Perhaps upset by the man's anger, he failed to take advantage of his good luck, and took a 6, to the par 4s of the others. Four behind Ouimet and three behind Vardon, he was now more or less out of the hunt and emphasised this by three-putting the short 16th.

It was clearly now Vardon *v* Ouimet as they teed up on the 17th, a dog-leg. One shot behind, Vardon took the risk of aiming for the angle of the dog-leg, hoping to set up a short pitch to the green. He hooked into a bunker where he had no shot at all to the green and a 5 was inevitable. Francis had driven straight and followed with a mid iron about 20ft past the pin. If he could just ease his putt up to the hole, the championship would be in his pocket. His putt died on the lip – and toppled in.

The 18th then became almost a formality. Vardon took a dispirited 6 and Ray's birdie came far too late. Francis was on in two and putted about 4ft short. The coma of calm in which he had played throughout now deserted Ouimet as the enormity of the achievement came to him for the first time. His knees and elbows trembled. He paused for a second or two and then got it into the hole. A 72 to Ray's 78 and Harry Vardon's 77. Their scores over the last nine, against a par of 3, 4, 4, 4, 5, 4, 3, 4, 4, were:

Ouimet   34 (3, 4, 4, 4, 5, 4, 3, 3, 4)
Vardon   39 (4, 4, 5, 3, 5, 4, 3, 5, 6)
Ray   40 (4, 4, 5, 4, 5, 6, 4, 5, 3)

American golf never again looked back. True, Ted Ray took the US Open in 1920 but no Englishman was to do so again for fifty years. Ouimet had foreshadowed the coming mastery of men such as Hagen, Sarazen and Jones and had shown that the best Britons could be beaten by a young man of twenty who, to be unkind, was only a good golfer – never again did he play quite as well as in that September of 1913.

The man who couldn't lose - the 1966 US Open

One of the quiet pleasures of looking back on Open Championships of the past comes from noticing an early appearance of an unknown, later to become one of the great players. There is the young Gary Player of the early 1950s, desperate to succeed but apparently blessed only with a hideous flat swing and a worse grip on the club. Or Walter Hagen getting his name spelled wrongly in a US Open before World War I. In the 1966 US Open Johnny Miller first attracted attention as a nineteen-year-old from Brigham Young University. He had come along to the Olympic Country Club in San Francisco to caddie, although he had attempted to qualify and was marked down as a substitute to compete in the championship in the event of late withdrawals.

There were withdrawals and he did play. In the first round he went round in 70, superb pitching already a feature of his game. This was good enough to put him near the head of the field and to command more than a fair share of press attention. Thereafter he slipped down the field a little, but it was a considerable achievement for someone who had never played with professionals before.

After the first round, another unknown led the field, Al

Page 103 Different pressures: *(above)* Lee Trevino and Tony Jacklin, 1972; *(below)* Arnold Palmer on his way to the first tee, Carnoustie, 1968

Page 104 Play-off, 1975: Watson and Newton before the ordeal at Carnoustie

Mengert on 67, but more eyes were on those considered to have a real chance of winning. Lema, Goalby, Marr, Nicklaus and Palmer all had 71s. Phil Rodgers was on 70 and Casper was one better; Littler had 68.

In the second round another unknown caused the stir. Ray McBee had improved on his first round by no fewer than twelve strokes to record a 64. This was an Open record and included nine birdies. Marr, Lema, Goalby and Mengert faded a little in their challenge, especially the latter who had a 77. It was beginning already to look like a battle amongst the four big names: Nicklaus, Casper, Palmer and Player, although the holder, Gary Player, had virtually ruled himself out with a 78. Palmer on the other hand had been in his best form and had gone round in 66 for a two-round total of 137 to lie equal first with Casper (69, 68). Rodgers was on 140, as was Ray McBee – but no one expected to hear much more of him. Nicklaus lay handily on 142.

Low-scoring rounds were few, for the course was of a kind that brings out latent claustrophobia in even the most uninhibited player. I think it is true to say that few of us have nightmares about bunkers set 220–60yd from the tee. We know that either we will not get that far or that we will lash the ball splendidly over them. We can even take careful aim at them – the best way of all to be sure of ending up somewhere quite different! But the Olympic course offered hazards of a different kind. For a start, the rough and semi-rough was springy and wiry. Because clubs so easily turned in the hands at impact it was a gamble to risk any straight-faced iron. So a tee shot that wandered from the narrow fairways often meant a stroke conceded to par – the golfer had either to wedge back to the fairway or, if he chose a bolder course, often saw his ball hiss through the grass for a handful of yards only. And, for good measure, he might even be behind a tree in the first place.

Trees, 20,000 of them, were the main hazard of the course. Very nice to look at – cypress, pine, eucalyptus – but the beauty became secondary when you were wondering if you could force a recovery shot over the top or find a gap to the green beyond. It got worse the further the golfer progressed in his round, for the last four holes were the most tree-menaced of all, ending with the 18th, a narrow tunnel leading to a green.

To keep it straight, then, was the important thing. Many took irons from the tee or at most a 3-wood, only to find that they lacked the ability to put the long iron shots that inevitably followed on to the green. This perhaps is why the US Open and British Open are seldom won by anyone not of the very highest class. The circuit golfer in America develops a game based primarily on three skills: long driving that need not be too scrupulously straight, mastery of the pitching wedge, and, as always, putting. Open courses call for all the shots and greater accuracy as well.

Some were able to adapt their game, mainly in taking a shorter, more controlled backswing and trying to fade their drives in from the left to the centre of the fairway as Nicklaus did.

In the third round Palmer had the better of his personal duel with Casper, and it was a contest given added colour by the contrast in personality and approach to the game. Palmer is nothing if not bold. He goes almost invariably for the long drive, the big carry and the flag. By 1966 he was perhaps less bold on the green. Casper, however, played the game almost in reverse. A quick, easy practice swing and the ball went straight down the middle a very reasonable distance; if then there was a carry over a water hazard he normally lay up short of it. Once on the green he was as aggressive as Palmer off it. Perhaps the best putter in the world since Bobby Locke, Casper counted on making up for lack of daring elsewhere with his wristy, relaxed putting stroke.

After six holes of the third round Palmer had a lead of four strokes on Casper, but they slipped away from him and the pair were all square again after thirteen. On the run in Palmer avoided trouble off the tee but found the rough or trees thereafter. Nevertheless he still salvaged two birdies and a par while dropping a stroke on the remaining two. Casper's steadiness was less in evidence than usual and his position weakened. At the end of the day Palmer led on 207, Casper, after a 73, was on 210 and Nicklaus's 69 saw him into third place on 211. The rest of the field was 213 or worse and did not figure prominently during the final round.

Neither did Nicklaus. He opened with a 6, failed to birdie any of the first nine holes, and was out of it. He finished with a 74 and 285 – good enough for third place.

The rest of the story belongs exclusively to Palmer and Casper. Palmer really made his reputation by coming from behind with a last-round 65 to win the US Open in 1960. That, and similar achievements in lesser tournaments, gave him a reputation for the 'charge'. In fact, after those early years, he seems more often to play his best golf on the front nine and then try to hold his round together from then in.

So it went that day. Palmer began with two birdies and added others to be out in 32. On the 10th Casper said to Palmer, 'I'm really going to have to go to get second, Arnie.' He was now seven strokes to the bad, his role seemingly to maintain his hold on second place and otherwise remain in the background while the main question was settled: Palmer was going to win but would he be able to beat Ben Hogan's eighteen-year-old US Open record? He needed a 68 and was well on the way to it. Par on the back nine would give him the record.

On the par-3 10th he missed the green and took 4 but parred the next and, with Casper, birdied the 12th. On the 13th, another par 3, he again took 4. The 14th passed in par and the record was still a possibility. Casper, unnoticed by the army that, as usual, followed Palmer, had been playing steadily and had picked up a couple of strokes on the leader. With four holes to play he was five strokes behind.

Palmer continued to handle the par 3s badly, and the 150yd 15th was another of them. He was bunkered with his 7-iron from the tee after going boldly for the flag and, though he came out well, failed to hole a 9ft putt. Casper, having played for the middle of the green, was down in 2.

Palmer said later, 'That's when I began to wonder. I knew what could happen.' The 16th was a monster, stretching 604yd. A long tee shot was needed to take some of the pressure off. Casper played safe with an iron from the tee; Palmer's drive, an attempt at a long hook, hit a cypress tree 180yd out after pulling sharply and his ball dropped down into the rye grass. He had to get distance, he felt, fingered a 3-iron, made up his mind, and swung. It skittered about 70yd into thicker rough. In the end, he did well to get a 6. But Casper, after three safe shots to the green, holed from some 6yd for a 4. Two holes, four strokes gone. Casper was now only one stroke behind.

Again Palmer's ball was in the rough from the 17th tee and again he could not force it out. This time it was a 6-iron that the springy grass twisted in his hands. Five for Palmer when his putt stopped 1in short, a 4 for Casper. All square with one hole to play.

The ending ought to be that a completely unnerved Palmer took several strokes too many on the last and that Billy Casper was then acclaimed champion. In fact both had pars after Palmer had again hooked into thick rough. It was all to play for the next day.

To look now at their scores in cold print – 71 to Palmer, Casper 68 – shows how little the mathematics tell the story on occasion. It looks as if Arnold Palmer had a nice steady round but that Casper was that important bit better. In reality, Palmer blundered badly and a couple of good putts by Casper finished him off. Ever since, it has been every leader's nightmare that he too should squander a similar lead – but then few have been quite that far ahead.

The play-off was not an anti-climax, although the pattern was grotesquely similar. Palmer reached the turn in 33 shots, although this time he did not leave his opponent trailing for Casper was only two strokes behind. The 12th was decisive. Casper found himself between files of cypress; Palmer was in the rough. Casper reached the green with his recovery and holed a 10yd putt; Palmer did not, and then missed a putt of little over a yard. Once again his lead was gone, and he went behind when Casper holed another long putt on the next. On the 14th Palmer was once again in the rough and one further behind. He then missed the 15th green from the tee and so came to the 604yd 16th three shots in arrears. Surely he would not play it so badly a second time?

He did worse. Again his drive caught a tree; again he took out the same 3-iron and this time managed to hack his ball little more than 20yd. It all ended in a 7. But this time Casper did have the grace to three-putt and promptly did so again at the next. Perhaps he too was flinching under the burden of a formidable lead. If so, his play on the final hole did not betray it. He was down the middle with his drive, put an iron about 3ft from the hole and duly holed out. Casper 69 to Palmer's 73.

So Billy Casper went down in the records as the 1966 Open Champion but the story remains how – or how on earth – Arnold Palmer managed to lose it.

Beauty and the Beast - the 1968 US Open

When Jack Fleck took the 1955 US Open out of Ben Hogan's hands – hands that were just about ready to reach out for the cup – he was an unknown. Afterwards he merged into obscurity once more, only occasionally earning brief recognition for some lesser achievement. We can see that Fleck must have been touched by some magic wand for that week at the Olympic Club.

In 1968, Lee Trevino was almost equally unknown. True, he had come up as a club assistant pro from a course no one had heard of and had finished fifth in the previous year's Open and had then had minor successes on the tour. This was much better than his $30 weekly club wage. But at the end of his best performance he had shown that he cracked under pressure – in one tournament he got himself into a winning position and hit weak iron shots on the last two holes. His swaying, flat, lunge of a swing completed the picture of a man who was nowhere near being championship material. They said the same thing about Walter Hagen.

Oak Hill, venue for the 1968 Open, is no terror of a course. Most observers felt that scoring would be on the low side. However, when play ended for the day on 13 June, only three players had broken par – Trevino, Charles Coody and Bert Yancey. Trevino had been fading nicely on to the fairway and had hardly missed one. With Coody he was on 69. Yancey had improved on his reputation of being one of the best putters of the day and led them both by two shots.

At the time, what caused more interest was how badly some of the others had played. On a course with a par of 70 it had seemed that an average of at least 69s would be needed to win but that any one of a number of players would probably put in the odd 65 or 66 somewhere. In fact the great names laboured. Nicklaus had 72, Palmer, 73, Sanders, 73, Bruce Crampton, 76, Bob Goalby – 'winner' of the Masters after Roberto de Vicenzo's mistake with his scorecard – 76, Frank Beard, 76 and Ken Venturi, 79. Perhaps the Open exerts unique pressures that are not much alleviated even by an easy course.

The next day Yancey carried on as he had begun, for a 68 this time. It gave him a record for the halfway stage of a US Open. Once again very few players had broken par. Charlie Sifford had 69 and Harold Henning of South Africa, 68, but they both had to balance these scores against 75s in the first round. Only Trevino was by now still near Yancey. He had missed just about every alternate fairway this time, but had still produced a good score by scrambling the ball to the green some-how and then showing what a good putter he was. He had a 68 to remain two shots behind. Otherwise, it looked as if Nicklaus, never to be discounted, on 142, might still be able to threaten Yancey but only if he could putt as well as the championship leader had been doing – fewer than 60 putts for the two rounds played.

The last two rounds were, in effect, matchplay: Yancey *v* Trevino. Yancey went out in 34, which was two shots better than Trevino, and increased his lead to four. This became five on the next hole.

The play on the 11th may well have been crucial psycho-logically. Yancey marked his ball a little to the side so that Trevino would not be distracted by his marker. Trevino holed for a birdie and Yancey replaced his ball directly behind his marker – forgetting that he had placed it a few inches away for Trevino's putt. If Trevino said nothing Yancey would earn a two-stroke penalty. Trevino reminded him. Virtue earned its reward at the next hole as Trevino birdied again and then repeated the feat on the 14th. When Yancey dropped a stroke on the 16th, his lead had melted to a single shot. At the end of the round, though his 70 had set another Open record – for a three-round total – he was by then only one shot better than Trevino. In matchplay terms, Trevino would start the second 18 one up from the boost of having broken Yancey's lead.

In terms of style it was Beauty against the Beast; Bert Yancey's classical upright swing against Trevino's roundhouse method. On another level it was the withdrawn, colourless personality against the crowd-pleasing antics and wise-cracking of Trevino. On the other hand, they started level in two respects: both had shown themselves to be master putters at their best; both had questionable temperaments.

Yancey had been a West Point cadet but had suffered a nervous breakdown that had kept him in hospital for nearly a year – hardly evidence of the kind of mental toughness needed to carry off an Open. But, despite what people say, golf is not life. The man you can always depend on to miss every important putt may be able to float through a vital business negotiation or come down Niagara in a barrel without a tremor. And vice versa.

Trevino, as mentioned, had failed before when faced with the near certainty of his first tournament win. Was his apparently relaxed manner a front to conceal the tensions within? Looking back with the benefit of later knowledge, we can see that Trevino does indeed use the extrovert in him as a shield. Where Hogan strode the fairways tightlipped and baleful eyed, attempting to sheathe himself from golf galleries, Trevino works off his tension with quips and clowning and is able to switch singlemindedly to the business in hand for the few seconds it takes to hit a golf shot. I have seen him break off in mid sentence while he hits a drive and then immediately pick up again once the ball has left his clubhead. Perhaps the tension is best expressed in the way he prowls around both green and tee before he hits and by the fact that there are far fewer jokes when Trevino is in with a chance in the last round. So it was that day, until Trevino relaxed when in an unassailable position.

Neither could have been mistaken for championship golfers on the early holes. They failed to get their pars on the 1st and Trevino had to scramble one on the next. On the 3rd Yancey missed just about his first short putt of the Open. He did it a second time on the 5th and was no longer in the lead. Trevino had his nose in front for the first time. But only for a few minutes, as Yancey got a birdie on the next hole. Nevertheless, at the turn Trevino, with a 36, led Yancey, 38, by one shot. Yancey then immediately hit one into trees from the 10th tee and went two strokes behind.

Now Yancey was down and Trevino quickly finished him off with birdies at the next two holes while Yancey gave him the present of another stroke by three-putting the 13th. For the round as a whole he took seven more shots than the new champion and so finished six behind, and even two behind Nicklaus, who had played yet another fine last round, a 67, which would have won him the championship if Trevino had weakened.

Trevino's victory put him firmly in the centre of the stage where he has stayed ever since. His swing? Well, Americans have never genuflected before the altar of style as the British tend to do. So, though it had been said no man could go far with a swing like *that*, success in the Open meant that Trevino's instructional articles and books soon sold as well as anybody else's. If your swing works . . .

High Drama

Return from the dead – the 1964 US Open

KEN VENTURI just could not win the Masters. While still an amateur in 1956, after rounds of 66, 69, 75, he went into the last round four shots ahead of the field. Could an amateur win the championship that the greatest amateur of them all, Bobby Jones, had founded? The answer was a final round of 80. He did not. The legend has become that Venturi's golf simply collapsed, but this was far from the case. The greens at Augusta that year were particularly fast and slippery – terrifying to putt on and very difficult to hold with the approach shot. Venturi again and again found himself just off the putting surface, chipped fairly close and then failed to hole the putts he had left.

Most of the field had similar problems in the winds of the final round and solved them no better than Venturi. Except for Jack Burke, who went round in 71 to win.

Two years later Venturi was playing with Palmer in the last round and coming home only one shot behind the soon-to-be great man. Again Venturi did not really collapse; Palmer eagled the 13th and that was just about that.

In 1960 Palmer turned up again. Venturi was back in the club-house with 283, having fought back after a poor opening round. Palmer was the man with a remote chance of catching him. He needed a birdie on one of the last two holes for a 283 total. He birdied them both.

Perhaps this was the straw that broke the camel's back. In the second half of the 1950s Venturi had steadily established himself as amongst the very best of American players. He had won two tournaments in 1957 and then three the following year. In 1960 he stood second in the list of money winners. In 1961 he was

14th. Worse was to follow. In 1962 he was 66th and then 94th, winning a derisory $3,848, in 1963.

His swing was gone. Once it had been described as an ideal balance of the controlled efficiency of Hogan and the perfection of rhythm of Snead. Balance was its essence and his set-up to the ball made striking look the most natural thing in the world. But by 1963, after trying to learn to hook for distance, he crouched down over the ball, snatched the club back too fast and too flat, went into a loop and then cut down across the ball from outside to in.

Other professionals on the circuit tried to help with advice but Ken Venturi seemed to pay little attention. A tip can be useful when a golfer is playing quite well but, for example, has the ball too far forward or back, or has his shoulders rather too open or closed, but Ken Venturi had probably reached that nadir when, by a last-moment reflex action, the hands flinch away from the ball. The only cure can be to await the time when a minor miracle occurs and the true path of the golf swing is suddenly there again. Meanwhile, he developed a stammer and facial twitches.

Others before him had arrived at the top and were then suddenly no more. Mike Souchak, after a string of successes on the US circuit, took too long a vacation and was never quite the same man again. Ralph Guldahl was winning everything in the late 1930s and woke up one morning to find that, though his method to every eye was the same, the right things were no longer quite happening to the ball. For most golfers it is the putting stroke that seems to suffer the most. This happened, amongst others, to Walter Hagen, Bobby Jones, when he came back from retirement to play in the Masters, and Ben Hogan, who in later years seemed to sweat over the impossibility of taking back his putter. One famous amateur, Count John de Bendern, stood turned to stone over *any* shot.

To go with the slump in his game, Venturi met other problems – scorecards incorrectly filled in, playing the wrong ball, a disc which popped out from time to time, and troubles with both hands and wrists. Of course his putting went too.

116

For three years running Venturi failed to qualify for the US Open, and in 1964, despite his previous high placings in that event, did not qualify for an invitation to the Masters either. Perhaps he could sink no further, for in the weeks preceding the 1964 Open he finished well up in a couple of tournaments. He came to the Congressional Country Club in 1966 in a better frame of mind but was obviously nobody's favourite to win.

The course was long – over 7,000yd – at the time the longest used in the championship, but the US PGA seemed to have been influenced by the frequent criticisms that the courses were made too tight from the tee. At Congressional the fairways were generously wide and virtually without bunkers. The rough had been burned by the sun and gave few any real problem. It was the greens which were the menace this time.

Their texture was strongly grained, as a result of the blend of grasses used. Against the grain, a ball had to be almost punched at the hole, and with it, merely setting the ball in motion was sometimes too much. Sidehill putts confounded some of the competitors – would the ball hold its line or bend through 90°? Sam Snead at the 4th in the first round took four putts, then three at the 6th before throwing his club into a water hazard.

The surfaces were hard and the traditional pattern of American golf of lofting iron shots at the flag and watching the ball bite and spin back had to be abandoned. This particularly suited Ken Venturi. At his best, he was a suspect putter and liable to hit the odd wild drive, but he was the best iron player in the business. He could vary the shape of the shot to suit the demands of the contours of the green, the pin position and the wind. He would draw one shot into the flag, float in another with fade or punch in a low 4-iron with a short flick of the wrists when others were lofting in 8- and 9-irons.

Venturi had a 72 in the first round and a lucky one at that. On one hole he had failed to get back to the fairway after driving far into the rough and had thrown away two shots with bunker play that would have disgraced a weekend golfer. In the second round the quality of his iron play began to show, and he finished a couple of strokes better.

But the talk was not of Venturi. Palmer had played the most consistent golf of anyone for 68, 69, and it looked as if he might repeat his success in the Masters earlier that year. He was not, however, in the lead. Tommy Jacobs had begun with 72 and in the second round had shown that it was just possible to plunder Congressional. He had played one of the great rounds of Open Championship golf history – 64. Even today, only Miller has bettered it with his 63 in the 1973 US Open. There was not much luck about his round except for his last stroke, a putt from the front of the green into the bottom of the hole. Otherwise he had hit sixteen greens in the right number of strokes and had usually put his ball close enough to hope for a birdie. He had got quite a few.

On this second day the temperature had been in the 90s and the humidity high. On the final day, with two rounds to play, the weather was much the same. At that time the US PGA and the British PGA both believed that their Open should test a man's physical endurance. Now, the higher takings from four days of competitive play have prevailed.

As play began, Jacobs led on 136, followed by Palmer one shot behind. Then there was a long gap to Bill Collins with 141. Next came the negro Charlie Sifford with 142 and Ken Venturi. Palmer is nothing if not tough and vital and, considering the demands that heat and humidity were going to make of a man, he was the clear favourite. On the opening holes he missed all the greens. In no time he was several shots behind Jacobs, who was playing without the unrepeatable brilliance of the previous day but very well. Venturi began with a putt for a birdie that hung half in, half out of the hole for an eternity. Then it fell in. Venturi must have felt that at long last the gods were favouring him again. After eight holes he had added three more birdies and parred the others. He was ahead of Palmer as he played the 9th, a 'proper' par 5. It measured 599yd and the green was fronted by a ravine. Venturi put his short pitch about 9ft from the hole and down went the putt. He was out in 30. On the 12th he added another birdie to be six strokes better than par. Jacobs's record was now beatable and Venturi led the championship.

There is some kind of special magic about the two halves of a golf course, even though nine is not a mystic number. If a golfer plays the first nine badly he will often experience a lift of spirits when he tackles the second. The recent past can be forgotten for the journey home to the clubhouse. Similarly, if he reaches the turn after a blaze of birdies he tends to feel that the round has become something to be defended against cruel assaults of fate on the perilous route home. These are reasons for the few rounds in the very low 60s.

Venturi, defending what he had already won, came back less dramatically in 36, which gave him a 66 and a three-round total of 208. This ought still to have been good enough to share the lead, and he would have but for missing two short putts at the end of his round. As it was, Tommy Jacobs had played the finer inward half – 34 – and held a two-shot lead on 206 after his round of 70. After his poor start, and for all the characteristic hitches of his slacks that signal determination, Arnold Palmer had not been able to make up ground. He had played more steadily later on but had managed not a single birdie. His 75 gave him a total of 212 and put him six strokes behind the leader.

In the clubhouse, Venturi offered an explanation – golfers always have at least one – for his seeming lack of resolution on the last holes. The heat and humidity had exhausted him, he said. A doctor saw him, told him not to eat, advised tea and, with salt tablets, accompanied him to the first tee and throughout the last round.

The 1964 US Open was by now a three-horse race with three basic questions waiting to be answered during the afternoon's play. Could Venturi keep on his feet and withstand thoughts of Palmer rampaging behind him? Could Palmer indeed stage yet another of his dazzling last-round performances and charge to the front? And what of Jacobs, the leader? He was known for occasional brilliance and daring rather than steadiness. So far in the championship he had shown both. Could he keep it up?

Venturi looked as if he would not last the round. His face was drawn and his walk laboured and stiff. Nevertheless, he parred seven of the first eight holes and no substantial threat had developed two holes behind from either Palmer or Jacobs. Palmer had begun with a birdie but had then dropped shots at two following holes. Jacobs had severely damaged his chances by taking 5 on a par 3.

As Venturi began to play the enormous 9th he was level with Jacobs. His drive was short but in no trouble and he followed it with a superbly struck 1-iron to within a whisker of the ravine in front of the green. Disregarding a bunker that threatened a few yards behind the flag he pitched boldly for it and holed the putt. The birdie put him in the lead.

In retrospect, this was the crucial hole. Venturi must have felt that he could stave off exhaustion long enough to get back to the clubhouse and leading an Open is a powerful stimulant to any golfer. He parred his way home while, behind him, both Palmer and Jacobs struggled to collect a couple of birdies. In going for their shots they had bogeys instead.

Ken Venturi was never to win a Masters but the US Open Championship is a good enough substitute for most men.

Beating the damned Yankees - the 1965 British Open

One reason for Bobby Jones's reputation resting on a peak that few others have felt it remotely possible to climb is that he won everything there was to win on both sides of the Atlantic. Similarly, Ben Hogan's perfect achievement, of competing in the British Open once and winning once, rounded off his record as even several other wins in the US Masters and Open could not have done. The reverse side of this particular coin is that Henry Cotton, arguably the best golfer in the world during the second half of the 1930s, did not compete in the USA in this period so the peak of his achievement is usually taken to be his 1937 British Open, when he beat the assembled might of the US Ryder Cup team – but that was under British conditions. It may be that he had little relish for US courses.

In the case of Peter Thomson there is no doubt at all. He does not like target golf – lofting pitch shots into well-watered greens in the knowledge that the ball will bite and stop. Consequently, he had won only one major US tournament and fourth was his best finish in the US Open or Masters. His record rested on his unmatched sequence during the 1950s in the British Open: 1952, second; 1953, joint second; 1954-6, winner; 1957, second; 1958, winner. Indeed, he and Bobby Locke in the immediate post-war period had made the British Open their own property. Locke, however, had also proved that he could beat the Americans, and on their own soil as well, with his famed rusty putter.

In 1960 Arnold Palmer had come to Britain for the first time, and from then on the British Open ceased to be the somewhat parochial event it had become, with British and Commonwealth players only competing. By 1965 the British Open was more an unofficial world championship than was the American competition. On balance, it attracted a more international entry.

In 1965 the American challenge was represented by twice-winner Palmer, Jack Nicklaus, the automatic favourite, Doug Sanders, 1964 winner, Tony Lema and Sam Snead who, as has now been the case for nearly twenty years, was thought too old to win. Other likely winners were the 1960 champion, Kel Nagle, Gary Player, Bob Charles, Bruce Devlin and Roberto de Vicenzo, who, surely, must pull it off sometime?

Thomson was given little chance before the championship began, although he had won at Royal Birkdale before – in 1954. Although still a young man at thirty-five, he was old in the wear and tear of competitive golf and had not finished higher than fifth since his last victory, over David Thomas in 1958.

Nevertheless the course suited his method of play. It was just over 7,000yd long, with five par 5s, which would normally have given a major advantage to those with maximum length from the tee – de Vicenzo, Palmer and, of course, Nicklaus, who in practice had reached the 510yd 17th with a sand wedge for his second shot! But the second nine, which contained four of these par 5s, was downwind throughout the championship: everyone could get up in two most of the time. Thomson has always been underpowered and, at the age of thirty-five, probably hit the ball less far than he had at his peak. But the course was hard and the ball ran a long way, often into thick rough and scrub. Thomson would score with his straightness from the tee and the precision of his long-iron play. Also, he is a master of the down-wind pitch, using the contours of the approaches to the greens rather than rely on the all-air route, as a Nicklaus or a Palmer prefers.

The first round put few out of contention. Bob Charles was gone after a 78, Player, having just won the US Open, had no better than a 76 and Doug Sanders had found out what the rough was like. He had a 9 on the 393yd 10th.

Lema, more or less just off the plane, as when he had won the previous year, led with a 68 made by good iron play and a few longish putts, followed by Christy O'Connor with a 69. Palmer was well up on 70, bracketed with the great Irish amateur, Joe Carr. Bruce Devlin followed with a 71.

On the second day, the leaders remained much the same:

140	Lema (68, 72)	142	Brown (72, 70)
	Devlin (71, 69)		Thomson (74, 68)
141	Palmer (70, 71)	143	De Vicenzo (74, 69)
	Huggett (73, 68)	144	Nicklaus, Will, Platts,
142	Boyle (73, 69)		Nagle
	O'Connor (69, 73)		
	Carr (70, 72)		

The British challenge was holding up better than usual, with five in the first nine. Nevertheless, most observers felt that the final rounds would be fought out amongst Lema, Devlin and Palmer. Few gave Huggett, who had been in poor form, any real chance of winning, even after his 68, which included an eagle and three birdies at par 5s, and Thomson, despite the round of the day, rarely won by coming from behind. His 68 had been made by improved putting and impeccably straight driving and long-iron play. His fellow Australian, Kel Nagle, had improved with a 70 but at forty-four years of age he probably could not sustain another major effort so soon after losing to Gary Player in the play-off for the US Open.

The 1965 British Open was the last occasion on which the final two rounds were played on one day. Thomson was paired with Lema, the man who, in the event, he had to fight for the championship. He began the day two shots behind the American, but after 45 holes had overtaken him to lead the tournament for the first time. The wind had become far stiffer, though by no means the kind of gale that is apt to scatter both players and tentage at British Opens. But it was enough to loft scores substantially. Huggett faltered to 76, Nicklaus to 77 and Palmer, Nagle, Devlin and – most important – Lema had 75s. Of those in serious contention, Thomson's 72 was the best round, nearly equalled only by de Vicenzo with 73.

In the afternoon Thomson began with a slim lead: one shot better than Lema and Devlin, two on Palmer, de Vicenzo and O'Connor, with Huggett one shot further away at 217. Going out before him were the men who would set a target to beat. Bernard Hunt was one of the first to do so. After a pair of 74s he played the best golf of anybody on the final day and finished 70 (the best third round), 71, but his total of 289 seemed three or four too many. De Vicenzo began well and looked for a while as if he might at long last win – until he took four putts from the front of the 9th green and finally finished his chances with drives into the rough on the last two holes. Despite these errors, he was round in 72 for 288. Playing round with him was Arnold Palmer, from whom there was this time nothing like a final charge. A 79 left him well out of it.

Thomson gave away nothing on the outward nine and reached the turn in 34. If he could come back steadily and ease in a few putts, the Open was at his mercy – providing his partner, Tony Lema, produced no fireworks.

The real crisis for both of them came after the turn. Thomson, from the 11th to the 14th respectively, failed to hole putts of 5, 2, 8 and 4ft. But Lema gained little on him. He had troubles of his own. He missed a very short putt for a 3 on the 190yd 12th, and on the next short hole, the 202yd 14th, he failed to note the strength of the wind around the green. It carried his ball away and he bogeyed the hole.

Apart from what Lema might do, it was now becoming clearer to Thomson what he had to do. It looked as if a 70 would easily be good enough and that he might be able to afford a shot or two more. In fact, O'Connor and Huggett sustained a challenge. The Irishman had a final 71 for 287 and Huggett gave himself the chance to win the Open when he holed long putts on both the 15th and 16th, but he approached both the 17th and 18th poorly. His final 70 put him level with O'Connor.

With five holes to go, Thomson was one shot ahead of Lema. With two to go, he knew that he had to get a 4 and a 5 to beat the rest of the field on two holes that each measured more than 500yd. Lema, on the other hand, needed at least two 4s to tie with Thomson. Thomson played the holes immaculately. On both he drove straight and then rifled a 3-iron into the green and was down in two more. Lema, who had fought so well through the three days, collapsed to 5, 6.

This had been a new Thomson. He is one of the few golfers who actually looks as if he is enjoying himself, has a word and a smile for the galleries, and is unwilling to admit that championship golf is the most important thing in life. To lose was not the end of the world and Thomson had won often enough to sate the ambition of most men. But he had not beaten the Americans, and some of them had used harsh words about his lack of power. So Thomson went round through the long day with an American and spoke hardly a word to him or anyone else. He was all cold determination.

He gained his victory and perhaps that was enough. True, nowadays he seldom misses an Open but he is there just for the occasion, as perhaps Palmer also. His greatest Open victory was his fifth and almost certainly his last. It equalled the five wins of J. H. Taylor and James Braid. Harry Vardon, as is right and proper, still stands alone on the ultimate peak.

'This one for the Open' - the 1970 British Open

The British are used to watching Americans, South Africans and Australians fighting out the closing stages of the Open amongst themselves. Most of the time it is as much as can be hoped for if a British player pulls out a good finishing round that drags him up the field to fourth place. But in July 1970 the best golfer in the world, on current form, was Tony Jacklin. He came to the 1970 British Open as the holder and three weeks before he had caused the British press to scurry across the Atlantic to view the final scenes when he took the US Open as well.

A golfer must capitalise on his commercial pull while he can, and Jacklin's manager, Mark McCormack, had given him a busy programme since his US Open win. In the days before he settled in at St Andrews he had been flying around Britain with Arnold Palmer playing a hole or two on one course and then on to another for a TV programme. Surely, the knowledgeable said, no way to prepare for a championship.

Jacklin went out on the first day and put a wedge shot to the 1st some dozen feet from the pin and holed the putt. At the next he was only 5ft away and again the putt went down. He was 15ft away at the next but again the putt was in. A steady par followed and he hit the green at the 567yd 5th with a 4-wood and two putts gave him another birdie. At the 7th he hit a drive about 320yd to an awkward spot on a bunker lip, gave the next shot a lot of thought and played a run-up to about a yard. He passed the 8th in par and played safe on the 359yd 9th by taking a 1-iron from the tee. He still had only a 9-iron to the green. The shot flew in at the pin, bounced twice, and went in. Well then, seven under par and out in 29. Palmer for years had shown he could stand the pace of a golf champion's life and here, too, was Jacklin showing no signs of wear and tear.

At the 10th he played a pitch and run to 6ft and holed the putt. The 11th was another par. The 12th was 312yd and during the championship Nicklaus put one tee shot 4ft from the hole. Jacklin's driving had been described as the best at the time amongst British and American players. His drive flew on line towards the green, pitched and bounced on towards it, only to strike a woman scorer and stop. His next shot would have to be a chip on, instead of an approach putt or a try for an eagle. His chip lacked precision but another par went down on the card, followed by another on the 13th. The 14th was another clear birdie opportunity as a 560yd par 5. Jacklin's drive had been a good one as the rain began to come down. He then lined up on the flag with a 4-wood. As he swung into the shot there was a shout of 'fore' from nearby. Jacklin flinched and came off the shot. His ball tailed away to the right and into a bush. At this point the Scottish weather took a hand in the proceedings.

The day had opened mild and with a sea mist that had delayed the start of play for half an hour. There was no wind. St Andrews is not a severe test of a top-class golfer in these conditions, neither perhaps is any links course. If the ground is firm a tee shot will bound on along the crisp turf so that most of the time, on even the longest par 4s, a good golfer needs only a pitch into the green; he has few doubts of his ability to reach the par 5s in two. But let the wind get up and the examination of his ability becomes severe. Any cut or draw he puts on the ball will first be accentuated by the wind and, when it pitches on green or fairway, the ball skips away sideways into rough, bunker, whin and hollow. True striking then becomes far more vital than on softer inland courses.

Most of the field made hay as the sun shone. No less than forty broke par in the first round while twenty-four of these were under 70. As the afternoon wore on, however, the sun stopped shining and the rains came. Soon the greens were under water and declared unplayable. Jacklin was still contemplating his ball in the bush as play was suspended for the rest of the day.

It was decided that the first round should not start again but that those who had not completed it should continue from where they had marked their balls the previous day. For Jacklin the moment had passed. He dropped out of the bush under penalty and went over par for the first time. Two more bogeys followed, though he got back to par once more on the last hole. But a likely 63 ended as a 67. Good in all conscience, but it left Neil Coles the first-round leader and new holder of the course record with 65.

Coles is a golfer of distinction, among the top British golfers for nearly two decades and also a man of character and some idiosyncrasy. He has a distaste for air travel, for looking like a model for golf clothing, and for links courses. The first of these problems he has solved by not competing in America (except in the Ryder Cup) or on other far-flung circuits and, when necessary, travels only by boat and car. Where Snead and Hogan covered their thinning pates decently with hat or cap, Coles allows his few long strands to fly in the wind, and while others stride confidently forward in thigh-hugging slacks of many hues and checks with matching sweaters, Coles strolls along in emphatically baggy trousers and very conservative cardigans. Bobby Locke's stately advance down the fairways gave him the nickname of 'The Archbishop'. Coles has not perhaps quite the presence for that, but has at least some of the attributes of an archdeacon. Certainly he would not look out of place in any pulpit in the land.

His distaste for links golf had meant that he had seldom distinguished himself in the Open. Park courses and Wentworth's Burma Road in particular were where he excelled. But that day at St Andrews he went out in 31 and like Jacklin holed a 9-iron second shot – in his case to the 364yd 7th. Unlike Jacklin he did not weaken on his way back.

There is little point, when so many made St Andrews look easy, in detailing other low scores. The main thing is that few of the fancied contenders had played themselves out of it. Nicklaus, Palmer, Trevino, Henning, Aaron, Bembridge and Horton were all round in 68 or better. So too was Sanders. His poor recent record had meant that he had had to qualify, and to watch him shape up to the ball was as agonising an experience as looking at Peter Oosterhuis. He would shuffle his feet and adjust his stance interminably before apparently giving the whole thing up with a final drastic shift of position. His swing, never a thing of much charm, was more stiff and mechanical than ever. 'But watch how he goes through the ball,' they used to say of him. Not any more. The convulsive, short jerk of the backswing was followed by a lurch which became a heave, with the whole performance ending inelegantly off balance. Still, handsome is as handsome does, and aided by a putter that was working well he had his 68,

despite hitting his second into the Swilken Burn at the 1st hole.
Sanders had a ready explanation for this error. He said his game
'isn't built around an early start'. It was unlikely, however, that
his out-of-tune swing would hold together as the wind came up
for the second round. The greens remained in perfect condition
– Trevino, daring the Nemesis that awaits all golfers who so
rashly challenge her, said 'You can't miss from 6ft.'

When the second round was over no one had yet grasped the
championship. Trevino, whose low-flying shots help make him
a good wind player, had a one-stroke lead on 136. Nicklaus
who had not won a major championship for three years, was in
second place with Jacklin. The latter could have been expected
to go round disconsolate in the mid 70s after the disappointments
that had marred his early-morning completion of the first
round, but he played steadily for his 70. On 139 were Henning,
Coles, who had only managed a 74, and Sanders. The British,
and the Scots in particular, are considered far better at the run-up
over seaside turf while Americans excel at lofting towering
wedges direct at the flag. But Doug Sanders has played a lot in
Britain, and it is doubtful if anyone is better than he at this shot,
which calls for touch and judgement of how the ball will run
over the ground between you and the flag, rather than merely
relying on a machine-like swing.

For the third round the course was a shot or two more difficult, and Trevino increased his lead to two shots after a 72. He
stood on 208, followed by a trio on 210 of Jacklin, Nicklaus and
Sanders, whose 71 was the best amongst those still in real contention (only twelve in the field beat par). Coles was on 211,
again playing as well as anyone, and a new face had appeared.
Oosterhuis had opened with 73, when strict par was certainly no
more than 70, but had followed this with a 69. His second 69
was the best round of the day.

Many consider that the third round is decisive – someone
leaves the rest gasping in his wake, a leader collapses to a 76. In
this case, however, the adjustments were minor: no one faltered
much; Sanders and Oosterhuis improved their position on the
leaders. There was all to play for in the last round.

The wind had steadily increased with each day of competition, and with it the scores, on paper, grew worse. On the final day it gusted to 65mph. The rape of St Andrews was over.

Let us talk for a moment of the difference the wind made by comparing the progress of three highly competent American golfers through the four rounds – Tommy Aaron, Dave Marr and Gay Brewer, who have each won a major championship. On the first day they all broke par with 68, 71 and 69. For the second round, when conditions were heavier, Marr alone broke par with another 71; Brewer and Aaron took 74s. On the third day Marr slipped a little to a 74 and Brewer had the same score. Aaron was gone – 79. On the final day none of them had any sort of answer to the conditions. Brewer and Aaron both took 80, Dave Marr 82.

How then did the leaders tackle the conditions? Trevino's putting stroke left him over the second nine and with it went his chances. Jacklin lasted a little longer but the two finished on 285 and 286 respectively with final rounds of 77 and 76. Henning made some sort of a challenge with a final 73 and was to be joint third with Trevino. Coles and Oosterhuis both had 76s for joint sixth place.

Nicklaus has fallen into the habit of caution. Let the rest risk all while he takes a 3-iron from the tee and attempts only the safe shot to the broadest areas of a green. In the final round, however, caution having not really paid off, he attempted to assert the real supremacy he has held for more than a decade. But perhaps fortune only favours the bold if they are bold all the time. He finished in 73 for 283 and waited for Doug Sanders, on the year's form a golfer two or three classes behind him, to win if he could.

In a sense the real story is that Sanders did in fact win it on the penultimate hole, the Road Hole. On this par 4 he bunkered his second shot by the green and had to come out strongly enough to be near the hole. But not too strongly, for then he would be on the road. He played the bunker shot of a lifetime to about 18in and holed the putt. Now he had only to play the comparatively simple par-4 18th in four shots to win. On the day its

358yd meant that you ought to hit a long drive in order to be left with a choice of shots: run it up through the Valley of Sin immediately in front of the green, or loft it over at the flag. Sanders hit an adequate drive. Obviously he was about to demonstrate once again, and finally, the mastery of the run-up he had shown all week. He had only to get the ball to within, say, 9ft of the pin and it was all over.

He decided to pitch. He abandoned his trust in being able to judge the strength of shot and the texture of the ground he had to run the ball over in favour of the usual American wedge at the flag.

But the Valley of Sin is old in experience of bringing doubts to the player of such a shot. Above all he must not be short and see the ball trickle back down the bank to his feet. Sanders went into the shot – still a simple enough one – and perhaps as impact neared he changed his mind. Some say he merely hit it too hard; others that the ball came through too low, indicating that he had come up on the shot, too eager to see just where it was going. It came to a stop 11 or 12yd past the hole. He was now left with a downhill putt. But it was still 'two for the Open'. To be over strong could mean a return to the Valley of Sin. Sanders was a little over cautious and his ball stopped 3–4ft from the hole. Now it was 'this one for the Open'.

The locals say that the putt Sanders was left with always breaks more from left to right, even from that distance, than you think. So it was. Sanders had to tap in for a tie with Jack Nicklaus.

He was little fancied in the play-off the following day. He had, despite being among the top ten money winners of all time, never taken a major championship. Nicklaus, on the other hand, had made a habit of it. But Nicklaus had problems too. He had not won for three years and a golfer at this level is only as good as his last Open, Masters or PGA.

After two holes they were level. Sanders three-putted the next to go one behind and found the rough at the next. Two behind. On the 5th he bunkered his tee shot and with his second just managed to get the ball out and no more. Sanders then put his 3-wood to the green on this 567yd par 5 into thick rough short of the green. But he got his par. To the turn both Nicklaus and Sanders then continued in par without particular drama: Sanders out in 38, Nicklaus, 36.

On the 11th Nicklaus went further ahead when Sanders took two to get out of sand and gained another stroke when Sanders was in the rough on the next. Four strokes up with six to go. Then Sanders birdied the 14th and 15th to halve the margin between them. On the 380yd 16th Nicklaus struck a 4-iron for his second that seemed to fly on and on. He needed three more to get down from through the green. The difference now was a single shot as they came to the Road Hole. Both drove well. Sanders played a 5-iron run-up to about 4½yd. Nicklaus hit a drawn and lofty 7-iron to a couple of yards less. Neither made a birdie; both were safely down in par 4s.

So, once again, it was all on the last. But this time Sanders had to get back a stroke from somewhere. He had the honour. If you watch his tee shot in normal or slow motion it is difficult to believe it was a good one. The laboured swing and convulsive heave is all there – but he still moved the ball to within about 30yd of the flag.

The hole measured 358yd but there was a wind behind. Nicklaus debated with himself whether or not a 3-wood might stop in the Valley of Sin while a driver might take him through the green. He decided on the driver and, in a gesture which – for Nicklaus – bordered on melodrama, discarded a sweater. His ball flew more or less on line and skipped on past the flag and on again into thick rough at the back of the green. It had travelled some 380yd and it is said that no one had previously driven through the back of the 18th at St Andrews.

This time Sanders did not pitch. He ran it up with nerveless touch – for someone trying to redeem the memories of earlier failure – to 4ft. Probably he would get his birdie this time. Now it was Nicklaus who had 'two for the Open'. First, he had a chip of about 25yd from the rough and then whatever putt he might be left with. The shot was downhill. Too firm, and it would run on down into the Valley of Sin; too weak, and there would be the prospect of having to wonder whether it was better to go boldly for the putt and risk missing the return. The championship now becomes the story of how Nicklaus won rather than how Sanders lost. Nicklaus chipped very well to about 8ft and was left with Sanders's problem of the day before. How much would it break right?

He misjudged the line a little, but not the strength. His putt caught the edge of the hole and toppled in. Sanders, at least, was spared having 'this one to tie for the Open' again.

Not how but how many – the 1972 British Open

To decide on the most dramatic of all Open Championships presents one with a choice from several candidates. To me, however, there is one that stands out as having all the ingredients, particularly of luck and tragedy, to an overwhelming extent – the 1972 British.

The protagonists who were the most closely involved in fighting it out were also very much as they should have been: Doug Sanders, having a go for it again after missing by 1in in 1970; Tony Jacklin, hope of the British crowds and twice an Open Champion; Lee Trevino, who had just lost his US Open title but came as the holder of the British; finally, Jack Nicklaus, who had already taken the US Masters and Open and was therefore once again in pursuit of the never-attained Grand Slam of Masters, US and British Opens and the US PGA.

The scene of the action was the 6,892yd of Muirfield. The course was in exceptional condition. Gary Player declared the greens, which had no automatic watering, to be magnificent. With his taste for hyperbole he said they were the best in the world. The fairways, under the unusual blazing sun, were hard and the aprons of the greens sometimes glazed in appearance. Shots hit without the ultimate in precision were going to skip into the rough and the small, deep pot bunkers for which the course is well known. Those of the players who were not frightened of the course in general were bothered by them: you could not ponder your lie in a fairway bunker, wondering if you would clear the lip and reach the green 150yd away. You were glad if you could get out, while hoping to move the ball forwards just a handful of yards.

Miller said that it was sometimes necessary to play out sideways; others were to wish they had when a ball trickled back to their feet. Doug Sanders summed it up well when he said, 'This course is lying there waiting for you.' Nicklaus, as a previous winner at Muirfield in 1966, had decided to play it the same way as he had then – defensively. When in doubt, he would take an iron from the tee. Provided he did not find the rough or a bunker, he could still get home, even at the par 5s, with a second iron shot. Such a strategy had worked for him in 1966. This time the defensive approach may have cost him the championship.

When play ended on the first day, the leader, as so often, was an unknown – Peter Tupling with a 68. One behind was Tony Jacklin and on 70, Jack Nicklaus. Several players were clustered on 71, including Trevino, Brian Barnes, Sanders and Player. Johnny Miller said he wished he had played out of bunkers sideways: he had 76.

The next day Miller showed himself at his best to a British crowd for the first time, and showed too that high-flying woods and irons did not put one at an insuperable disadvantage. His play on the 558yd 5th had done him no harm at all. After his drive he struck a wooden-club shot full at the flag and in it went for a double eagle, three under par. He finished in 66 and from nowhere was in joint third place. But the Miller of 1972 did not perhaps have quite the belief in himself that he now has. Today, if playing well, he expects to collect such scores and sees no reason why he should not do it again and again. This year he was to drift a little to 72 in the third round, which left him still with an outside chance of winning, but a final 75 meant that he finished well down.

At the end of the second day Jacklin and Trevino shared the lead on 141 and it was to remain more or less like that for the rest of the championship. The day's hard-luck story belonged to Doug Sanders. He had come to the 447yd 18th needing a 4 for a 68. He drove into a bunker, came out into rough, went on into another bunker . . . in the end there was a 7 to go down on his card. Instead of being two shots in the lead he was one behind. Tony Jacklin had had the same kind of troubles on the 153yd 13th. He too had gone from bunker to bunker en route to a 6. Three over par on one hole meant that the rest of his round had been very good indeed. Nicklaus's problems had come from his putting and he had three-putted in one stretch no less than three times in four holes. Nevertheless, he was only a shot behind the leaders, victory as yet by no means beyond his reach. The events of the third day were to make it seem so.

Jacklin played superbly well for a 67 that was made early on by a 3 on the 558yd 5th. He had the edge on Trevino, his playing partner, on nearly every hole, though Trevino was level par, 36, to the turn and continued with par figures until he came to the 14th. He birdied that one and all the rest, and all his putts – if he putted, that is – were from more than 6yd.

On the 14th he got one down from about this distance and followed with a putt of near double the length on the 396yd 15th. At the 16th he missed the green with his tee shot and was bunkered to the right. The shot left him little chance of keeping to par. His ball lay on a downward slope and there was little room between him and the flag to allow him space for his ball to run. Trevino played a bad shot, probably lifting his head too soon, and thinned it off the edge of his sand wedge rather than lobbing it into the air. His ball bounced short of the flag and skipped on, headed for the other side of the green and another bunker shot. Then it hit the flag flush in the middle and dropped down dead into the hole. He returned to normality on the 542yd 17th which he reached in two and then conventionally two-putted. But he was back in the groove again at the last. Through the green with his approach, he lay on the back fringe, some 10yd from the hole. The chip went in and Trevino had a 66 and now led the championship by one stroke from Jacklin – left to reflect on the lead *he* might have had. Four behind was Sanders and Nicklaus was six to the bad. Brian Barnes was five behind with 212.

To most observers, Jacklin was now the clear favourite. He had produced some of his best golf and had not let himself be stunned by Trevino's improvised magic, magic that was not likely to be repeated. Nicklaus might produce yet another final round of a lifetime but, provided Jacklin could produce par figures, this still ought not to be enough for a win.

At last Nicklaus attacked Muirfield, a course he had said during pre-tournament practice could not be attacked. Playing about two holes ahead of Jacklin and Trevino, he left them in no doubt that they had to do more than fight out the 1972 Open between themselves. He was out in 32 – four shots better than par – and when he birdied the 473yd par-4 10th he led the tournament.

A few minutes later Nicklaus was on the 11th green, Jacklin and Trevino on the 9th. Trevino holed from 6yd for an eagle and Jacklin followed him in from 9ft for another. Ahead, Nicklaus got his birdie. Thirty-eight shots for eleven holes. Thereafter his putts did not drop. He missed from 9ft at the 12th and failed to make birdies on each of the 13th, 14th and 15th. At the 16th, a 188yd par 3, he faltered. His tee shot hit the front edge of the green and kicked into the rough. He took three more shots to get down. On the next he hooked from the tee and was forced by his lie to play out on to the fairway rather than go for the green on this 542yd hole, which he would play as a par 4 – a drive and a 7-iron had got him there in an earlier round. He finished with a par and a 66 that remains one of the great might-have-beens of golf history. During it he had missed five putts of between 5 and 12ft but he had still set a formidable target. Jacklin needed a 70 to beat him, Trevino 71.

Nicklaus's par at the 17th had been a relative failure, and the hole settled the championship for Jacklin and Trevino as well. Trevino was checked when about to drive by a TV cameraman and then bunkered his shot. Jacklin drove long and straight. Trevino recovered from the bunker but his ball was still behind Jacklin's. His next shot with a 3-wood was short, to the left, and in thick rough. If Jacklin could now get his long second near the hole the championship would be his, and a birdie would almost certainly do it as well (he was one shot behind Trevino at this stage but it looked as if the best Trevino would be able to manage now was a 6).

Jacklin hit a good wooden-club shot but his ball came to rest well short of the green. Nevertheless he was left with only a short pitch, with the terrain between him and the flag presenting no problem. He struck it cleanly but perhaps with the merest suggestion of caution. He had left himself short and a birdie would now be difficult to get.

Trevino, however, was through the green in four. He walked up to his ball and, though always quick into the shot, seemed to play his chip carelessly – as if he felt the 1972 Open had slipped away from him. But there was one more chip shot left in him, a casual one or not. It ran towards the hole at the right pace and dropped in. Instead of the possible 7 and certain 6, Trevino had parred the hole in a way that would have caused any weekend golfer to apologise for his good luck.

Jacklin had now to hole his putt to draw level with Trevino. It ran briskly towards the hole and then on 3ft or so past.

When he had holed the chip, Trevino said, 'That may be the straw that breaks the camel's back.' Nicklaus's too for that matter, but he had not been with Trevino throughout two rounds to see the straws mount up as Jacklin had. Whether or not his back was broken, Tony Jacklin's 3ft putt was always off line.

For Trevino there was still Nicklaus to beat. He had to par the 447yd 18th to do it. He paused to let Jacklin get to the tee first so that he could move into his drive without any pause for self doubt. Away it went, leaving him about 150yd to the green. His second shot came in well. Two putts and Trevino was Open Champion for the second year running. Jacklin, all passion spent, bunkered his shot to the green and took three more to hole out.

So they finished:

278   Trevino (71, 70, 66, 71)
279   Nicklaus (70, 72, 71, 66)
280   Jacklin (69, 72, 67, 72)
281   Sanders (71, 71, 69, 70)

For Nicklaus, no Grand Slam this year; for Jacklin, a 'what-should-have-been' to think over for a decade or two; for Trevino, confirmation that in golf it is not 'how' but 'how many'.

Almost anyone's Open – the 1975 British Open

During the practice days before the 1975 Open began, the talk was of Nicklaus's run of 67, 65, 67, 65. He had won the US Masters, in a finish involving Weiskopf and Miller that is already a golfing legend, and had come very close in the US Open just previously. He would have to attack in this championship, for it was evident that Carnoustie, burnt up and windless, would yield good scores to golfers other than he. Any very good golfer who attacked boldly might pull it off. Nicklaus, despite the splendour of power that deceives, is a defensive player. Peter Dobereiner, writing in the *Observer*, put it succinctly: 'Most of the time he plays with the timidity of a middle-aged spinster walking home through a town full of drunken sailors, always choosing the safe side of the street. Sometimes he gets home safely. But more often he gets grabbed.'

Nicklaus began as if he had used up his good golf in practice. He found the first green with his second shot but then pulled his birdie putt badly. At the 2nd he thinned a chip and three-putted; at the 3rd he left himself a nasty 3ft putt but managed to get it down; at the 379yd 4th, which has a double green, he sank a long, long putt of at least 20yd for a birdie. The Great One was again himself. From this hole to the 12th he was four under par. He holed another huge putt for an eagle on the 488yd 14th, before a birdie at the next. He now faced the three finishing holes, which were to be the key to the championship.

The 235yd 16th with its narrow, bunker-flanked green was a difficult target. The difficulty is doubled by the fact that any shot that fails to bite in the centre of the green is thrown off by its convex shape. Nicklaus used a long iron and hit the green, but his ball just toppled off to the left and down.

The 17th, under the conditions in which the Open was played, was arguably the most difficult hole on the course. From the tee, two twists of the Barry Burn confront the player. If his name is Nicklaus he may hope to clear both and set up a short iron to the green. As far as I know, Nicklaus included, no one attempted the carry. They all took a long iron, aiming to clear the first meander but stop short of the second. Now there were two routes to the green. You either played left, pitched short and counted on swinging round through a gap on to the green, or sent a high-flying shot over the mounds and bunkers direct at the flag. If you did not fly it quite far enough you were in a pot bunker. Nicklaus got his 4.

From the 18th tee, the Barry Burn again had to be crossed twice before the green was reached: first it had to be carried with the drive and then again when it fronted the green. Nicklaus found a bunker to the right of the green, came out to 9ft and missed the putt. Two over par then for the last three holes, a pattern frequently repeated by others. Nevertheless, he had a 69 in his pocket – an unlikely prospect when he had lined up that huge putt on the 4th.

The rest of the first day was left to the funny names: Ooster-huis, Oosthuizen and Huish. Throughout the championship British eyes were focused mainly on the first of these.

Oosterhuis, who had finished as runner-up at Royal Lytham and St Annes the previous year, led the field with 68. Ooster-huis is two quite distinct players. Once near enough to the green to rely on touch rather than technique he can scuffle the ball up dead to the flag from the middle of any tuft of grass, bush or bunker that happens to be around. But watch him take a long shot. An observer from Mars would think swinging at a golf ball with admittedly peculiar-looking tools a highly unnatural and foredoomed activity.

For a start, Oosterhuis is obviously too tall for the project. The little white ball is an impossible distance away from the eye 6½ft above that is striving to keep it in focus. Moreover, where is the player to put his feet? He edges them this way and that and, in the due course of time, arrives at a final position that seems remarkably similar to where he began the whole manoeuvre.

By the 14th Oosterhuis may have been wondering when his particular bogey was going to appear, this being a push or slice – sometimes a combination of the two – of grand proportions. From the 15th tee he carved one away to the right and on to the adjoining 4th fairway. A fortunate escape, but it was a 5. On then to the 16th, where his 1-iron hit the green and then ran down the bank and away. Oosterhuis chipped it straight into the hole and moved on to the 17th much refreshed. No push this time and he was 12ft or so from the hole in two and down went the putt. Suddenly he found himself five under par and no one was matching those figures. Then came another prodigious slice at the last hole and another 5, but nevertheless he had a 68, a championship record for Carnoustie, matching Ben Hogan's winning final round in 1953.

Oosthuizen's name was prominent through the day, even though few could pronounce it, and he came to the last tee needing a 4 to share the lead. If he had done it, two of the most unlikely sounding names in world golf would have given head-line writers something to think about. But he put his second shot into a bunker and had to be content with a 69. With five others, he shared second place.

David Huish, a club professional at North Berwick, was one of these. He plays only a handful of tournaments during the year but had recently won the Scottish professional championship. Despite this, he had been required to qualify and had done so with nothing to spare. At one hole he lost a ball in a bush and took 8. Not content with that disaster he drove out of bounds a few holes later. But on the last green he holed a 12ft putt for a birdie and a sudden-death play-off with seven others. Huish drove the 1st green and was in.

That birdie spell was still there when he began at Carnoustie. He birdied the 1st, then hit a 4-iron a couple of inches from the hole at the 464yd 2nd and went on to birdie the 3rd as well. Three holes played, three under par. A little shocked perhaps by so unlikely a start, he played the next three holes in 5 apiece but was still out in 34 and came back steadily in 35. Perhaps because David Huish is a Scotsman, there was no problem over the

1*   139

pronunciation of *his* name – 'Hush', of course. (Of course?)

The others on 69 were Jack Newton and Bob Shearer of Australia and Hale Irwin. Irwin had played a dramatic round: two over par after five holes, he birdied seven of the next ten and at one of them, the 488yd 14th, he had hit the flag-stick with his wood into the green (a blind shot for everyone) and had then missed the eagle putt of rather less than a yard.

On 70 there were Hobday, Edwards, Leonard and Tapie, and on 71 Miller, de Vicenzo, Burns, Barnes, Cahill, Watson, Floyd and Mahaffey. A few of the big names seemed out of it already: Trevino with 76, Player, Lanny Wadkins and Gene Littler with 75, and, perhaps, Palmer and Charles with 74s. It certainly looked as if it was likely to be fatal to have dropped far behind while conditions were so easy. Everyone knows that it blows just about every day of the year at Carnoustie. Where was that wind?

Instead, it rained hard during night, which made the greens medium paced, while they became very receptive to incoming shots. Again there was hardly a breath of wind all day. The target golfers, who like to fly their shots in high at the flag and see them bite and stop, ought to have a field day. They did. The previous course record of 68 was beaten time and again.

One man who did not beat it was Peter Oosterhuis. He went out in 31 and followed that thrust with a par and then his sixth birdie of the day. He did not get another genuine* par until the 18th, and it added up to a second half of 39. Against strict par he had dropped six shots between the 12th and the 17th. After the 11th, he was looking for something like a 64; his 70 by the end of the day put him two strokes behind the leader, though still joint second.

The man who was two strokes in the lead was David Huish, and highly delighted about it. It is by no means rare for a 'minor' golfer to lead a major championship field after one round, but

---

* The 12th measures 478yd and the 14th is 488yd. Unless there is a headwind no professional, in the conditions prevailing, would see these holes as anything more than par 4s. Oosterhuis took 5 at each.

lightning, even of a benevolent kind, does not often strike twice.

Huish had begun with a 5. 'Oh dear,' they said, 'there he goes.' But not at all. He holed from 20ft at the 2nd for a birdie, did much the same thing at the 5th, after a birdie at the 4th, and was out in 34. Could he keep it up? On the return he holed some good putts, got his regulation birdies at the par 5s, but saved his final gem for the 16th. For this 235yd hole he took out a driver, put his ball on the green and holed a putt of about 7yd. He was round in 67.

The only golfer to better this was Bobby Cole, who had finished well up in the previous British Open. A shortened position of the left thumb, however, was going to make all the difference this year. Cole claimed it made his method firmer at the top of his backswing and prevented the club going past the horizontal. Cole had also come near to playing a perfect putting round. He had birdied each of the par 5s, two of the three par 3s on the card and two par 4s. After his opening 72 he had pushed up into joint second place, together with Oosterhuis, Oosthuizen and Tom Watson. Watson had followed a sound 71 with a 67. He too had birdied all the 5s on the card and had picked up four others.

Undoubtedly it was this ease with which the long holes could be played in four shots that was taming Carnoustie, making strict par no more than 69. A howl had gone up at Hazeltine National at the 1970 US Open when no one could reach the long holes in two shots; at Carnoustie the howl should have been that *everyone* could.

Other players besides Huish were causing surprise by having produced two good rounds in a row. One was the Irishman Leonard, even more of an unknown that Huish. One feature of his style is individualistic. The basis of his putting method is to separate the hands, putting the right only a few inches above the head of the club. The result – for some – is the feeling that the right hand is bowling the ball at the hole. Most of us, however, champions or not, are afraid of looking ridiculous, let alone grotesque. I cannot conceive, for instance, of a Hogan or Nicklaus risking titters from the galleries as a result of putting with any technique more original than elegant. But the several people who followed Leonard around saw him hole out very steadily indeed with this split-hands method. If he had won perhaps even Nicklaus would have turned his thoughts upon the techniques required, and then we would all have been doing it! But Leonard did not win the 1975 Open, though he did keep going commendably over the full four rounds. He added a 73 and a 74 to 70, 69 and finished on 286. That was worth £1,750, a lot more than the likes of Weiskopf, Player, Trevino and Palmer took back home with them.

And, alas, alas, for David Huish. Perhaps content with the thought that he would be able to tell his grandchildren all about 'How I led the Open after 36 holes', he first subsided to a 76 and worse followed on the final day – only two players who had got that far scored higher than his 80.

The third day usually sorts them out, but not so at Carnoustie in 1975. The boys were getting used to the idea that strict par really was no more than 69: anyone who did not beat the rated par of 72 this day put himself finally out of contention and there were eight who scored below 69.

One of them equalled the best score ever returned in a British Open: Jack Newton, with 65. He had taken some advice from Jack Nicklaus about setting his hands higher up on the putter and trying to get the feel of having his forearms in the stroke. Well, the only fixed rules about putting are that if it does not work it is no good and if it does, believe in it. Newton believed. He holed from several yards at the 1st and then from not much less at the 3rd and picked up one more birdie while going out in 32. At that point he faltered, putting his next shot to the green into a bunker. He came out well but his putt to save a par was weak and short. Taking an iron from the tee at the 372yd 11th, he headed for trouble but ended in a good lie and birdied the hole. Three more followed in succession and Newton passed the difficult 461yd 15th in par. Now for that final stretch.

At the 235yd 16th he pushed his drive and his little pitch shot failed to get quite to the putting surface. From the fringe Newton put his next one into the hole and was visibly delighted. Nor less so after the 17th, where he was safely on in two and then holed out from about 7yd. As he stood on the last tee a birdie would have beaten the Open Championship record round of 65 set by Henry Cotton at Sandwich in 1934. That round, coupled with a first round of 67, had left the rest looking about them to see who they would have to beat for second prize. Newton's did not even give him the lead.

Cole's short left thumb* was still working very well indeed, thank you, and one of the most fluid swings in golf had taken him round in another 66 to give him the lead.

At one point Tom Watson had led. He had begun par, birdie, birdie, birdie, par, birdie (this last one very nearly an eagle after he had struck a superb 3-wood into the 524yd 6th). Two more pars followed but then at the 9th he drove out of bounds to the left. Watson had been pleased with the way he had changed his natural game and, like Nicklaus, was hitting the long shots with a right-to-left drift. But Nicklaus *does* hook sometimes, and so did Watson now. He seemed not unduly shaken, however, got a par with his second ball, and went on to pick up three more birdies by the time he had reached the 16th tee. On this long par 3 he missed the green for the third time running and took 4 before dropping another shot on the last to finish on 69 for a three-round total of 207.

But the golfer attracting more attention than anyone else was Johnny Miller. There was the feeling that it was just about time that he won the British Open and memories were fresh of his two brilliant closing rounds in the 1975 US Masters. After them, and the earlier drama of his last-round 63 in the 1973 US Open, everyone tends to be waiting for him to do it again. At Carnoustie, the conditions were ideal for Miller's pattern of shot: both the greens and the fairways were holding his high-flying woods and

---

* I'm still trying to work this one out. Cole had apparently withdrawn his left thumb up the shaft so that it *no longer showed between his right thumb and forefinger.* 'Ah yes,' I said to myself, picking up a golf club to investigate this particular secret. My thumb, however, refused to show at all until I Vardoned no less than three fingers. Perhaps you have to have a long thumb to be able to shorten it?

irons. There was no need to play the manufactured, thought-out, running shots that Miller has yet to learn. He began by holing from about 5yd and then 6yd on the first two greens and, already, there was a good round in the making. On the 397yd 5th he then floated in an 8-iron from the sparse rough to a yard from the hole. At the long 6th he did not reach the green in two but chipped and putted for a birdie and then missed the green at the 7th. No matter. He got it into the hole from 4yd off. That made it three successive birdies and five in the seven holes played. He was in the lead for the first time and maintained his position to the turn. Out in 31, a total for the first half equalled only by Oosterhuis on the second day.

On the 10th Miller encountered trouble for the first time, finding one of the few little patches of rough that survived at Carnoustie. He was back to par at the next and now there came the two holes that, in retrospect, Miller may feel cost him the 1975 Open. The 12th was one of those short-playing par 5s that everyone was gobbling up. In two shots Miller was a touch short but still near enough to putt for an eagle. He went at the hole with the aggression he displayed throughout, shaved the hole, and stopped about 5ft past. He missed the return – an opportunity gone. Another went as he missed for a 2 at the 166yd 13th.

But he made no mistake at the 488yd 14th, where his 5-iron second found the green and his putt was a hair's breadth short of an eagle. He played the last four holes in level par. That was a 66 and a three-round total of 206 – two shots behind Cole, one behind Newton. Miller's secret? He had shifted his right hand a fraction more 'under' the shaft and this tautened his shot-making.

As the final day began, this is how they stood:

204 Cole
205 Newton
206 Miller
207 Watson
208 Irwin, Nicklaus, Coles, Mahaffey and Oosthuizen

(Oosthuizen, a twenty-one-year-old South African, had impetuously gone for the green when bunkered on the last but reached only the Barry Burn. To finish with a 6 leaves a sour taste in the mouth. Oosthuizen faded from sight the next day – but everyone now knew how to pronounce his name.)

It was still anybody's championship. Miller had been made favourite because only he of the four leaders had won an Open Championship, but he was joined by Nicklaus on the final morning because, at last, there was a wind and the pin positions were more severe, placed closer to protecting bunkers and on trickier areas of greens. Moreover, most holes were now stretched to their full length.

The wind made the outward half play longer. It would help later but the critical last three holes were not made substantially easier. The players had become just a little too accustomed to the conditions that had prevailed so far. In the wind, only Watson got to the turn under par and then by only a single shot. He threw that one and a couple of others away when he three-putted the 10th, 11th and 12th. It looked as if he could safely be forgotten.

Miller gave himself a jolt at the 1st hole. He went boldly at a very long putt, spun off the hole and finished a few feet away. He did not get the next putt in and made up no ground with birdies going out, though he dropped no more strokes.

Nicklaus also did not prosper to the turn. He missed a rather short putt at the 524yd 6th (no longer yielding routine birdies playing into the wind), put a poor tee shot into a bunker on the next, and made another mistake on the 9th. That was 38 to the turn and probably too much ground to make up.

Newton started more steadily than anyone, with four pars and a birdie on the first five holes. Then he took 6 on the 6th and immediately dropped a further stroke on the 7th. Completing his outward half with no more alarms, he stood one over par. On the next five holes he never went over par and birdied the two long holes. At this point, he looked to be the winner by about two strokes if he could play the last four in par.

And what of the overnight leader, Bobby Cole of South

Africa? As far back as 1966 he had won the Amateur Championship at Carnoustie, but for year on year thereafter had not ful-
filled the glittering prospects that had been forecast for him.
Then, in 1974, he had become a truly major golfer. Though still
to take a major championship, he had threatened to do so in the
1974 British Open and the US PGA, had come close to winning
his first US tour event, and had won the South African Open
after a last round of 64. Towards the end of the year he had won
something that perhaps *ought* to rank as high as an Open title –
the individual title in the World Cup. On the last day at Carnoustie Cole went out steadily.

As they came into the finishing stretch from the 14th, there
were really five in it: Newton, Cole, Nicklaus, Miller and
Watson. Even to specify only these five is to oversimplify. There
were others – Graham Marsh, Neil Coles, Oosterhuis, Mahaffey
and Irwin – who could all conceivably have taken the championship with a late surge. Nicklaus, Watson and Miller had to pick
up the odd stroke on par while Cole and Newton, following the
rest of the field, had only to maintain their position, rather than
die in attempting too-stirring deeds.

Let us now see how they dealt with those final holes.

Nicklaus got one in from a couple of yards for a birdie at the
14th and thus gained ground; Cole, on the other hand, missed
the green with a 5-iron from a perfect fairway position and
finished in a bunker: Newton got his 4, as did Watson.

At the 15th, Nicklaus had a second putt of 8ft to get in for his
par but did so; Watson put his second shot just slightly nearer
the hole than this but failed; Miller just missed the green on the
right but was safely down with a chip and putt. Cole pushed an
8-iron far to the right into the crowd. That was another shot
gone. Newton ran through the green, pulled his chip a little and
needed two putts.

Nobody played the 16th perfectly. Cole did best. He had a
putt of 6ft or so for a birdie and that might well have given him
the lift to surmount the difficulties and tensions of the last two
holes. But the putt did not go in. Newton put his tee shot into a
bunker and came out too short of the hole to have much chance

of holing his putt. Watson played the worst tee shot of the lot (this cannot be his favourite hole at Carnoustie: never once did he master the problem of hitting a straight shot over 200yd). This time he squirted or thinned a shot away to the right and into the crowd. He was at least 30yd from the green – a shot a long-handicapper would seek excuses for. Watson followed with a good pitch but did not hole the putt.

Miller and Nicklaus both parred the 17th, as did Watson, though in his case there was first a sliced iron shot to the green to be retrieved with a chip and putt. Neither Newton nor Cole had anything to be proud of in their tee shots at this hole, which was playing into the wind. Cole mishit and was almost in the Barry Burn. He then found he had a wood shot to play from a lie where the ball was very much above his feet. He hit it out of the heel and had dropped another shot. Newton chose the wrong club. Did he not realise that the carry over the first meander of the Barry Burn was made much longer by the stiff breeze or had he temporarily lost trust in his woods? It was a 2-iron he selected. He cleared the burn, but by a matter of inches only, so that his ball came to rest on the far bank and from there he could not hope to reach the green at this 454yd hole. Both he and Cole pitched well but missed their putts.

As they faced the last hole Newton and Miller needed a par for 279 whereas the three others needed a birdie to make this total.

Nicklaus and Miller played first, into a fresh crosswind. Nicklaus was safely down the fairway and Miller also hit what looked like a superb drive – a little too much towards the bunkers on the right but he had allowed for that: the wind would bring his ball back. It did not. The ball caught the edge of a bunker, followed it around and dropped in. No one at all relishes their chances of hitting a long bunker shot particularly close to a distant hole, so there had gone the 1975 British Open as far as Miller was concerned. Nevertheless, he decided to give it a go, believing that he needed a birdie: he did not know that Cole and Newton were having problems of their own on the 17th. Miller selected a 6-iron and hit his ball into the bunker face. If but once . . . He tried again. This time the shot came off: he finished a little to the left of the green but no great distance from the hole. His chip did not go in and he tapped in for a 5 and a total of 280. Nicklaus's approach was strong and went through the back. His chip looked dangerous all the way but in the end it was a par and the same total as Miller's.

Behind them Watson had observed the dramas ahead as he waited to play his approach shot. He put it safely on and had a putt of about 15ft for a birdie. There is very little to say about a putt of this length. It can be good (ie goes into the hole); quite good (finishes near); or poor (does not finish near). Tom Watson and all who watched him will remember his putt as very good indeed, and suddenly he had jumped into a position where Cole and Newton had to equal his total.

Cole had to equal Watson's birdie to tie with him; Newton had only to par. Both drove well and safely. Newton took the shot to the green first and his approach was about the same distance from the hole as Watson's. Cole took his time about it, walking to the green, and even after this examination, consulting with his caddie about choice of club. The decision at last made, he played quickly and decisively and finished about a yard nearer than Newton.

Newton now faced a putting problem that many of us would not mind having to face: shall I go for it and, if it goes in, be Open Champion or shall I prod it towards the hole and make sure of the tie? To me it seemed he decided to settle for future glory tomorrow rather than joy today: his approach putt was tentative. It could not have worried the watching Watson as it made its way towards the hole to stop a couple of feet away. Cole's turn now, and for him no mental conflict. It had to go in. It did not quite and he had to settle for £3,866 – but no mantle of champion. Newton carefully pushed his in.

So the real battle ended in a tie between Tom Watson and Jack Newton, but in this 1975 British Open there seemed no reason why the Sunday's play-off should not have been among another half dozen or so. If we now look at how they finished we can see that of the top fourteen only Graham Marsh, Bob

Charles and George Burns had needed a really low-scoring last round to finish top of the heap:

279	Watson	(71, 67, 69, 72)
	Newton	(69, 71, 65, 74)
280	Cole	(72, 66, 66, 76)
	Miller	(71, 69, 66, 74)
	Nicklaus	(69, 71, 68, 72)
281	Marsh	(72, 67, 71, 71)
282	Oosterhuis	(68, 70, 71, 73)
	Coles	(72, 69, 67, 74)
283	Irwin	(69, 70, 69, 75)
284	Burns	(71, 73, 69, 71)
	Mahaffey	(71, 68, 69, 76)
286	Charles	(74, 73, 70, 69)
	Leonard	(70, 69, 73, 74)
	Oosthuizen	(69, 69, 70, 78)

You could extend this list even further. Both Scotland's Bernard Gallacher and Alan Tapie (who?) of the US would also have won had they shot respectively a 67 and a 69.

Of course Saturday was not the final day. Watson and Newton had still to fight it out, but the essence of the 1975 Open is that Saturday afternoon's scramble when more players could have won than in any Open Championship, British or American, that has yet been played.

For the record, Watson beat Newton eventually by parring the final hole comfortably, while Newton bunkered his approach shot and did not.

Acknowledgements

CONTEMPORARY newspaper accounts have been particularly useful to me, especially as they give far fuller accounts of the play of people who did *not* win that do later writings in book form. They are also the best source for the full scores of the whole field – particularly so for the times long past when everyone had to play a couple of qualifying rounds before the championship proper began. Those that I have found the most useful are *The Times* and *The Sunday Times*, the *Guardian*, *Daily Telegraph* and *Observer*, the *New York Times* and the *New Yorker* Magazine.

The books that I have found helpful appear below. While not one of them is in any sense a record of Open Championships, they provide much useful detail.

Photographs
   Author and publishers gratefully acknowledge these agencies for the following photographs:
Associated Press – 8. Fox Photos – 2a, b, 5b. E. D. Lacey, 16 Post House Lane, Great Bookham, Surrey – 3a, b, 4a, b, 5a, c, 6a. Press Association – 1a, b, c, 2c, 7b. Sport and General – 6b. *The Times* – 7a.

Select Bibliography

(Unless otherwise stated, UK editions are listed and place of publication is London)

Alliss, P. and Ferrier, B. *Alliss through the looking-glass* (1963).
Cotton, H. *This game of golf* (1948).
Darwin, B. *Golf between two wars* (1944).
Gallico, P. *Farewell to sport*, New York (1937).
Hagen, W. *The Walter Hagen story* (1957).
Jones, R. T. jun and Keeler, O. B. *Down the fairway* (1927).
Jones, R. T. *Golf is my game* (1961).
——. *Bobby Jones on golf* (1968).
Longhurst, H. *Round in 68* (1953).
——. *My life and soft times* (1971).
McCormack, M. *The world of professional golf* , 8 vols (1968–75).
——. *Arnold Palmer – the man and the legend* (1967).
Murphy, M. *Golf in the Kingdom* (1974).
Nicklaus, J. and Wind, H. W. *The greatest game of all* (1969).
Plimpton, G. *The bogey man* (1967).
Price, C. *The world of golf* (1963).
Sarazen, E. and Wind, H. W. *Thirty years of championship golf*, Englewood Cliffs (1950).
Snead, S. *The education of a golfer* (1962).
Thomson, P. and Zwar, D. *This wonderful world of golf* (1969).
Ward-Thomas, P. *Masters of golf* (1960).
——. *The long, green fairway* (1966).
Wind, H. W. *The story of American golf*, New York (1956).
——. *The lure of golf* (1971).

Index

Numbers in italic type refer to illustrations

The championships

British Opens

US Opens